Elvis Presley

Titles in the
People Who Made History Series

People Who Made History

Elvis
Presley

James D. Torr, *Book Editor*

Bonnie Szumski, *Editorial Director*
Scott Barbour, *Managing Editor*
David M. Haugen, *Series Editor*

Greenhaven Press, Inc., San Diego, California

Every effort has been made to trace the owners of copyrighted material. The articles in this volume may have been edited for content, length, and/or reading level. The titles have been changed to enhance the editorial purpose. Those interested in locating the original source will find the complete citation on the first page of each article.

Library of Congress Cataloging-in-Publication Data

Elvis Presley / James D. Torr, book editor.
    p. cm. — (People who made history)
   Includes bibliographical references and indexes.
   ISBN 0-7377-0643-0 (pbk. : alk. paper)—
ISBN 0-7377-0644-9 (lib. bdg. : alk. paper)
   1. Presley, Elvis, 1935–1977. 2. Rock musicians—
United States—Biography. I. Torr, James D., 1974–
II. Series.

ML420.P96 E378 2001
782.42166'092—dc21   00-064680
[B]   CIP

Cover photo: © Shooting Star
Library of Congress, 21, 74, 81, 87, 117, 105, 129

Copyright © 2001 by Greenhaven Press, Inc.
PO Box 289009
San Diego, CA 92198-9009
Printed in the U.S.A.

CONTENTS

1956 he had signed with a major record label, appeared on television, and released several Top 40 radio hits. Elvis mania had swept the nation.

Chapter 4: Isolation and Decline

Chapter 5: Long Live the King

FOREWORD

In the vast and colorful pageant of human history, a handful of individuals stand out. They are the men and women who have come variously to be called "great," "leading," "brilliant," "pivotal," or "infamous" because they and their deeds forever changed their own society or the world as a whole. some were political or military leaders—kings, queens, presidents, generals, and the like—whose policies, conquests, or innovations reshaped the maps and futures of countries and entire continents. Among those falling into this category were the formidable Roman statesman/general Julius Caesar, who extended Rome's power into Gaul (what is now France); Caesar's lover and ally, the notorious Egyptian queen Cleopatra, who challenged the strongest male rules of her day; and England's stalwart Queen Elizabeth I, whose defeat of the mighty Spanish Armada saved England from subjugation.

Some of history's other movers and shakers were scientists or other thinkers whose ideas and discoveries altered the way people conduct their everyday lives or view themselves and their place in nature. The electric light and other remarkable inventions of Thomas Edison, for example, revolutionized almost every aspect of home-life and the workplace; and the theories of naturalist Charles Darwin lit the way for biologists and other scientists in their ongoing efforts to understand origins of living things, including human beings.

Still other people who made history were religious leaders and social reformers. The struggles of the Arabic prophet Muhammad more than a thousand years ago led to the establishment of one of the world's great religions—Islam; and the efforts and personal sacrifices of an American reverend named Martin Luther King Jr. brought about major improvements in race relations and the justice system in the United States.

Each anthology in the People Who Made History series begins with an introductory essay that provides a general overview of the individual's life, times, and contributions. The group of essays that follow are chose for their accessibility to a young adult audience and carefully edited in consideration of the reading and comprehension levels of that audience. Some of the essays are by noted historians, professors, and other experts. Others are excerpts from contemporary writings by or about the pivotal individual in question. To aid the reader in choosing the material of immediate interest or need, an annotated table of contents summarizes the article's main themes and insights.

Each volume also contains extensive research tools, including a collection of excerpts from primary source documents pertaining to the individual under discussion. The volumes are rounded out with an extensive bibliography and a comprehensive index.

Plutarch, the renowned first-century Greek biographer and moralist, crystallized the idea behind Greehaven's People Who Made History when he said, "To be ignorant of the lives of the most celebrated men of past ages is to continue in a state of childhood all our days." Indeed, since it is people who make history, every modern nation, organization, institution, invention, artifact, and idea is the result of the diligent efforts of one or more individuals, living or dead; and it is therefore impossible to understand how the world we live in came to be without examining the contributions of these individuals.

ELVIS PRESLEY: THE KING OF ROCK AND ROLL

In her book, *The Ultimate Elvis,* Patricia Jobe Pierce proclaims, "Nineteen fifty-four signals a turning point in American history." In 1954, Dwight D. Eisenhower was president. Senator Joe McCarthy was falsely accusing many Americans of being Communists. The Supreme Court ruled that racial segregation in public schools was unconstitutional. RCA had just introduced the color television. And, Pierce writes,

> In 1954, Elvis cracked open what is now labeled "the generation gap" with his sexual, macho image and his chaotic sound. Elvis created chasms that transformed the performing and visual arts by capturing the imagination of the masses and accomplished what few artists dared to express. Not only did he enliven the music scene, he gave direction, energy, and shape to what was to become the Age of Rock 'n' Roll.[1]

He is certainly the most famous entertainer in American history. As Jeff Pike, author of *The Death of Rock 'n' Roll,* notes, Elvis

> became the biggest thing ever in show business. Some claim the Beatles were bigger, but forget it. In terms of practically any criteria you want to use—chart action, record sales, name familiarity, lasting influence—Elvis was the biggest. Period. You need a degree in math to talk about it he was so big. Here's just one piece of it: he spent nearly half of 1956, nearly twenty-five weeks, with a record in the number 1 position on the pop chart, with "Heartbreak Hotel" (number 1 for eight weeks), "I Want You, I Need You, I Love You," "Don't Be Cruel" b/w "Hound Dog." . . . Then he repeated the stunt in 1957 (yes, that's right, another twenty-five weeks at number 1) with "Too Much," "All Shook Up," "(Let Me Be Your) Teddy Bear," and "Jailhouse Rock" b/w "Treat Me Nice."[2]

Elvis Presley had 110 titles, albums, and singles certified as gold, platinum, or multi-platinum—more than twice as many as the Beatles. Elvis has had more than twice as many Top 40 hits as any other artist or group since 1955.

But Elvis was more than just a singer. He was the embodiment of the musical and social revolution that was rock and roll. His very existence—a poor, relatively uneducated southern boy who had risen to become one of the most famous men in America—inspired a generation. Amidst the conformity of the 1950s, Elvis defied society's norms. He incorporated elements of black rhythm and blues into his music, he dressed outrageously, he moved onstage in ways that other white singers of his day didn't dare—and millions of teenagers loved him for it. He had such an effect on American culture that an estimated 300 music and sociology college courses around the country are devoted exclusively to Elvis. This is no surprise, for, as Kevin Quain, editor of *The Elvis Reader,* explains, "If you want to understand America, sooner or later you're going to have to deal with Elvis."[3]

ELVIS'S PARENTS

Elvis's parents, Vernon Presley and Gladys Smith Presley, were married in 1933, at the height of the Great Depression. In his book *Elvis,* rock biographer Dave Marsh describes Elvis's parents as average southerners:

> Vernon and Gladys Presley were typical Mississippians of their generation. . . . [They] came from farming families—when they were married, Vernon was still sharecropping with his father. In 1935, they had moved to town, Vernon driving trucks for a dairy and wholesale grocery, Gladys working at the Tupelo Garment Company as a sewing machine operator. Like so many others during the Depression, they were rural people in the process of becoming, if not urbanized, at least estranged from the soil.[4]

Vernon and Gladys worked twelve hours a day, six days a week, and between them earned $26 dollars a week. They lived in a small two-room house, with no running water, that Vernon and his father had built in 1934. "[Vernon and Gladys] were typical of their class and it was a constant struggle to avoid being categorized as the 'poor white trash' scorned by all facets of society,"[5] writes Rupert Matthews in his biography of Elvis.

Accounts of Elvis's early life vary with regard to how the Presleys' poverty affected their social standing in East Tupelo. As Marsh puts it, "the question of whether Elvis grew up 'white trash,'" became "a matter of some controversy once he became known outside the South."[6] Many biographers emphasize how hardworking both parents were, while others note that the Presleys occasionally lived on welfare and suffered an embarrassment in 1938 when Vernon was briefly imprisoned for passing a forged check. Vernon Presley commented on the family's hardscrabble years in Tupelo shortly before he died: "There were times we had nothing to eat but corn bread and water, . . . but we always had compassion for people. Poor we were, I'll never deny that. But trash we weren't. . . . We never had any prejudice. We never put anybody down. Neither did Elvis."[7] Of his impoverished upbringing Elvis once said simply, "We were broke, man, broke."[8]

Gladys Presley gave birth to Elvis on January 8, 1935, in the house Vernon had built. Elvis was born a twin, but his brother, Jesse, was stillborn. " 'We matched their names,' Mrs. Presley said years later. 'Jesse Garon and Elvis Aron.' "[9] Throughout his life Elvis spoke of his brother Jesse as watching over him from Heaven.

A Religious Upbringing

Religion played a major role in Elvis's childhood, and it was at church that Elvis seems to have developed his love of music. In keeping with southern tradition, the Presleys were evangelical Protestants, and in Tupelo they belonged to the First Assembly of God Church, a Pentecostal church. On Sundays the Presleys enjoyed singing along with the congregation, and the choir delighted young Elvis. Gladys recalled, "When Elvis was just a little fellow, he would slide off my lap, run down the aisle, and scramble up to the platform of the church. He would stand looking up at the choir and try to sing with them. He was too little to know the words, of course, but he could carry the tune."[10] "When I was four or five," Elvis later reminisced, "all I looked forward to was Sundays, when we all could go to church. This was the only singing training I ever had."[11]

Elvis's love of gospel music continued throughout his life. As a teenager he became a fan of gospel quartets such as the Statesmen Quartet and the Blackwood Brothers, and later in his career he often performed spirituals and toured with gospel groups. Many fans were surprised in 1957—when Elvis was already being referred to as the King of Rock and Roll—at his response to a reporter's question about what type of music he preferred to sing. Elvis responded, "My first love is spiritual music—some of the old colored spirituals from way back."[12]

Elvis the child soon began singing outside the church walls. When he was in the fifth grade he won second prize at the Mississippi-Alabama Fair and Dairy Show for singing "Old Shep," a song about a boy and his dog, and for his eleventh birthday Elvis received a guitar. But perhaps the most important step in Elvis's musical development came in September 1948, when the Presleys moved from Tupelo to Memphis, Tennessee.

THE MEMPHIS BLUES

The Presleys made the move to Memphis solely for financial reasons: When the family came on hard times in Tupelo in 1948, Vernon hoped to find work in Memphis's much larger economy. At first, though, life was harder in Memphis. Vernon didn't find a good-paying job for months, and the shy, thirteen-year-old Elvis was slow to fit in at his new school. The Presleys could only afford a single room, sharing a kitchen and bathroom with three other families. But according to biographers Peter Harry Brown and Pat H. Broeske, the difficult move had unforeseen benefits for Elvis's musical ambitions:

> For a budding young musician, he couldn't have moved to a better city. Memphis was a mecca of musical influences.
>
> Just half a mile to the south was Beale Street, that brightly lit, tanked-up home of the blues. Among those who had performed there were Louis Armstrong, Big Mama Thornton, and Dinah Shore. . . .
>
> Meanwhile, the sounds of gospel echoed throughout the city's countless churches and meeting halls and spilled out onto the streets. Roadhouses hosted hillbilly bands from the Ozarks and cowboy singers from Nashville.[13]

Elvis biographers generally agree that Memphis was where Elvis received the most exposure to black rhythm and blues (R&B). The South's first black radio station, WDIA, had been established in Memphis in 1948, and featured bluesmen B.B. King and Rufus Thomas as singer/disc jockeys. Elvis later claimed to have listened to the station constantly. And Memphis's Beale Street afforded Elvis the opportunity to hear the blues firsthand. According to Marsh, "His taste was forming as he took in the country blues of Arthur 'Big Boy' Crudup and Big Bill Broonzy, the more urbane shouting of Roy Brown and Wynonie Harris, the rawer New Orleans music of Lloyd Price and Fats Domino."[14] "There is no question that Elvis was well acquainted with the rhythm and blues sound," writes Patsy Guy Hammontree in *Elvis Presley: A Bio-Bibliography.* "He could not have grown up in the Memphis area without hearing a great deal of 'soul' music."[15]

Marsh, Hammontree, and most other Elvis biographers place so much emphasis on the blues scene in Memphis because the musical genre that Elvis would soon make famous—rock and roll—was very heavily influenced by black R&B. "Black rhythm and blues was ad-libbed and spontaneous," writes Pierce. "Rhythm and blues is mournful, honest, and direct. Many songs deal with becoming emancipated from slavery of any kind. It's kind of from the gut."[16] The gospel music that Elvis loved was also heavily influenced by black artists. Commenting on Elvis's later success, rock critic Robert G. Pielke writes, "It's worth remembering that none of it would have happened had not Elvis been familiar with black music as well as white. . . . Elvis was white, but he clearly sounded black—a heady brew for folks at the time."[17]

Despite the influence that the Memphis blues scene seems to have had on him, there is little evidence that Elvis had any ambitions of becoming a bluesman. In high school Elvis often sang for his friends, but the only other times he expressed an interest in singing in public were when he spoke of wanting to join a gospel quartet. If he had a greater ambition, it was probably to become a ballad singer like Dean Martin and the other mainstream white entertainers of his day. Though as a teenager Elvis had begun to develop a rather loud appearance—he sported sideburns and often dressed in pink or yellow sportcoats—he was hardly a rebel. In the racially segregated 1950s, the thought of intentionally violating longstanding social taboos by singing the blues probably never crossed Elvis's mind.

ROCKABILLY

The type of music that Elvis first became famous for was known as rockabilly—a cross between country music and R&B, the two genres of music indigenous to the American South. The origins of the music predated Elvis's first success.

"Bill Haley put them together with his cover of Sonny Dae's 'Rock Around the Clock' in 1954,"[18] writes Pielke. However, Haley had gone on to form a country band, the Saddlemen, thus distancing himself from R&B audiences. Black performers such as Fats Domino or Chuck Berry had also pioneered the rockabilly sound, but in the 1950s they were not accepted enough by mainstream white audiences. Sam Phillips, the founder of Sun Record Company in Memphis, had made a name for himself promoting black R&B artists, but he was aware that, to make the new music more than a fad among mainstream America, "A fusion had to take place; a white boy had to sing the blues,"[19] as music critic Michael Bane puts it.

Elvis graduated from high school on June 14, 1953. He first took a job as a factory worker at the Precision Tool Company, and a few weeks later became a truck driver and warehouse worker at the Crown Electric Company. Then one day in July 1953, on his lunch hour, Elvis walked into the Memphis Recording Studio—a sideline to the Sun Record Company—where anyone could pay to make their own record, two songs for four dollars. He recorded a ballad, "My Happiness," and a 1951 hit by the Ink Spots, "That's Where Your Heartaches Begin." Marion Keisker, who recorded Elvis's performance that day, made a tape copy of his record and wrote down the words "Good ballad singer. Hold." Months later Sam Phillips called Elvis into the studio to make his first commercial recordings.

THE RISE TO FAME

Elvis received his call from Sun Records in June 1954. Phillips had Elvis record four songs with guitarist Scotty Moore and bassist Bill Black, who became Elvis's band and his friends for the next few years. At first the trio got off to a rough start. Elvis wanted to sing ballads but Phillips insisted on something that would appeal to younger audiences. Finally they launched into a speeded-up version of Arthur "Big Boy" Crudup's "That's All Right Mama." Brown and Boeske describe the scene: "Listening to the playbacks, they knew they had something unique. Elvis's voice was a mesmerizing mix of gospel, the low, gravelly growls of country, and a startlingly 'black' sound. 'Good God!' said Moore. 'They'll run us out of town when they hear this!'"[20]

On July 7, the record received its first play on Memphis's WHBQ. According to Robert G. Pielke, author of *You Say You*

Want a Revolution: Rock Music in American Culture, disc jockey Dewey Phillips (no relation to Sam) "had to play it repeatedly all evening, and was finally compelled to have someone drag Elvis out of a local movie theater for a live interview."[21] Within days, Sun had received orders for 5,000 copies of the new record and offered Elvis a recording contract.

Things happened quickly after that. "That's All Right Mama" went to number one on the local country charts, and the group, calling themselves The Hillbilly Cat and the Blue Moon Boys, started touring. It took the new performer a few shows to overcome his stage fright, but Elvis soon embraced the spotlight, driving audiences of screaming teenagers wild. In September Elvis released a second single, "Good Rockin' Tonight," and in October he appeared on the local television program *Louisiana Hayride.* After his first performance the show signed Elvis to a year-long contract; he appeared every Saturday night. By November Elvis was making enough money performing that he quit his job as a truck driver.

During this time Elvis was already developing his unique onstage persona—the outrageous clothing, the good-natured smile that could quickly become a cynical sneer, and the extraordinary gyrations that drove his female fans wild. "Everybody was screaming . . . my manager told me it was because I was wigglin'," he once said. "Well, I went back for an encore and I did a little more."[22] "It is difficult for us, after years of exposure to pop shows full of dancing and physical mobility, to realize just how astonishing Elvis was when he first appeared on stage," writes Matthews. "Until that time singers were expected to be quite static. Stars such as Bing Crosby stood in front of a microphone and just sang."[23] Elvis, on the other hand, would wave his arms, shake his leg, and sway—or sometimes convulsively jerk—his hips.

The first of many "Elvis riots" occurred at a Jacksonville, Florida, concert on May 13, 1955. After his usual exhilarating performance, Elvis grinned to the girls in the crowd of 14,000 and said, "Girls, I'll see y'all backstage."[24] Hundreds stormed the backstage area and when the pandemonium finally died down, Elvis's jacket and shirt had been ripped off, his shoes had been taken, he was bruised, and his Cadillac had been covered in lipstick. Eventually the hysteria that followed Elvis's performances would become a cause for concern among parents nationwide. But in 1955, the immediate effect of all this excitement was to attract the attention of a new manager, Colonel Tom Parker.

THE COLONEL

The Colonel (an honorary title given to him by the governor of Virginia) is one of the most mysterious and controversial figures in Elvis's life. His real name was Andreas Cornelius van Kuijk. He was born in the Netherlands and changed his name after coming to America in 1929. At first he earned quite a reputation as a carnival and circus promoter—reportedly his schemes included painting sparrows yellow and selling them as canaries and creating a "dancing chicken" act by heating the bottoms of the birds' cages. By the 1950s he had begun managing several country singers, and in 1955 he turned his full attention to Elvis. The Colonel formally became Elvis's manager in March 1956.

The influence that the Colonel exerted over Elvis in their 22 years together is debatable. Most biographers feel that the Colonel put his own financial concerns before Elvis's best interests. For example, in the 1960s the Colonel convinced Elvis to give him 50 percent of his earnings, when the industry standard was 15 to 25 percent. But the Colonel also helped Elvis to become one of the most famous entertainers in history.

The Colonel's first step was to ingratiate himself with Elvis's parents. Once he had their approval, Elvis readily agreed to let the Colonel manage his career. The Colonel convinced Vernon and Gladys that Elvis needed to leave Sun and sign with a larger record label (under Sun Elvis's singles were only being played on southern radio stations). Through the summer and fall of 1955, as Elvis continued to tour and record, the Colonel negotiated the deal in which Sam Phillips sold Elvis's contract to RCA Victor for $40,000, the largest amount ever paid for a pop vocalist.

At RCA Victor, Elvis's material would receive national airplay. As Paul Friedlander writes in *Rock and Roll: A Social History,* "The stage was set. . . . The rock artist, the major label, the crafty manager, the quality studio, and its legendary musicians were about to deliver the first rock deity. On January 10, 1956, Elvis entered RCA's Nashville studios . . . to record 'Heartbreak Hotel' and 'I Want You, I Need You, I Love You.' "[25] "Heartbreak Hotel" became Elvis's breakaway hit, going to number one on *Billboard*'s list of national Top 40 hits. Elvis would have 21 more Top 40 hits with RCA in the next four years.

The next step in the Colonel's plan was to generate publicity for the rising star, which meant television appearances. Elvis made his national television debut on January 28, 1956, on the Dorsey Brothers' *Stage Show.* He followed this with April and June appearances on the *Milton Berle Show,* and in July pulled 55 percent of the viewing audience when he appeared on the *Steve Allen Show.* Elvis's most famous TV appearance, however, came on September 9 on *The Ed Sullivan Show.*

Sullivan had initially refused to have a rock and roller such as Elvis on the show, but faced with the high ratings of Elvis's *Steve Allen* appearance, Sullivan finally acquiesced. He insisted, however, that Elvis be filmed only from the waist up, feeling that Elvis's gyrations were unfit for a family audience. Elvis's censored performance attracted 54 million viewers. In his biography of Elvis, David Rubel writes, "That kind of number was unheard of. President Eisenhower's speech accepting the 1956 Republican presidential nomination carried on all three networks had attracted only fifty-one million viewers. It was a record."[26]

THE BACKLASH AGAINST ELVIS MANIA

With *The Ed Sullivan Show,* Elvis mania had begun in earnest, though not everyone was pleased about it. Marsh writes, "It wasn't his records that ultimately made Elvis Presley a household dream and nightmare; it was those wild-eyed TV performances of his records, sheer, paralyzing intensity brought straight into comfortable homes."[27] Critics nationwide immediately attacked Elvis's onstage gyrations as being sexually suggestive and inappropriate for young audiences. Jack O'Brien's review in the New York *Journal-American* was typical:

> Elvis Presley wiggled and wiggled with such abdominal gyrations that burlesque bombshell Georgia Southern really deserves equal time to reply in gyrating kind. He can't sing a lick, makes up for vocal shortcomings with the weirdest and plainly planned, suggestive animation short of an aborigine's mating dance.[28]

By all accounts, Elvis was confused and often upset about these attacks. He continually maintained that he was simply dancing onstage: "My arms and legs just follow the music,"[29] he responded to one of the countless interview questions about his "suggestive" movements.

In retrospect, many historians argue that the backlash against Elvis was directed at more than just his dancing. "Fear of increasing juvenile delinquency underlay much of the backlash against Presley," writes David P. Szatmary in his history of rock and roll. Movies like *The Wild One* (1954) and *Rebel Without a Cause* (1955) had been preying on a national scare about teen violence, and many adults associated rock and roll with images of teens banding together and causing mayhem.

Moreover, many of the attacks on Elvis were directed not so much at the singer but what he represented: the new teen movement centered around rock and roll. In the 1950s, writes Pierce, "Teenagers were bored, ignored, and eager to find something to glorify and revere. . . . [Elvis's] wild performances broke from the bland American mainstream of 'Ozzie and Harriet' or 'Father Knows Best' and the oppressed, youthful minority went wild over this raunchy, flagrantly sexual boy from the wrong side of the tracks."[30]

And while rock and roll had been around for a few years before Elvis appeared on *The Ed Sullivan Show,* Pielke believes it was Elvis's casual disregard for society's taboos about race, class, and sex that helped give rock its element of rebellion:

> Before Elvis there were rich and vital musical traditions among both blacks and whites, but there was no revolution. Before Elvis there was even something called rock and roll, but there was no revolution. Before Elvis there was rage and alienation throughout the entire country, barely held in check by a dogmatically repressive and subtly authoritarian regime, yet still there was no revolution. . . . Hence, as John Lennon observed on hearing about his death at Graceland, "Before Elvis, there was nobody."[31]

Despite the status of "rebel" that was foisted upon him, Elvis probably never wanted to ignite the fires of teen rebellion. He simply wanted to sing—and to act in the movies as well. In the fall of 1956, even as the controversy was erupting over the now legendary *Ed Sullivan* appearance, Elvis was happily filming his first movie, *Love Me Tender.* His records were dominating the pop charts, with five number one hits and seven more in the Top 40 in 1956 alone. In 1957 he bought the thirteen-room Graceland mansion and filmed two more movies, *Loving You* and

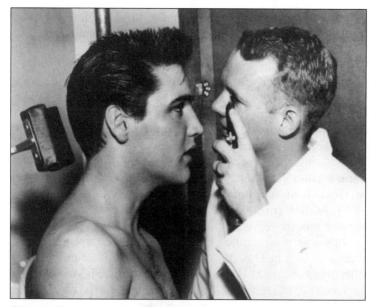

Elvis Presley receives his army physical in March 1958. Despite offers of preferential treatment, Presley wanted to be "a regular GI."

Jailhouse Rock. The King of Rock and Roll was at the height of his reign.

G.I. BLUES

It was not to last. Elvis received his draft notice on December 20, 1957. The King of Rock and Roll still had to answer to Uncle Sam. Some Elvis aficionados insist that the draft was the U.S. government's way of putting Elvis "in his place." Others believe that the Colonel was concerned that Elvis's image as rebel might make him less profitable. They speculate that Parker saw military service as way of cleaning up Elvis's image, and may have pulled strings with the army recruiters in Memphis.

Whatever the case, Elvis was inducted into the U.S. Army on March 24, 1958. He received a sixty-day deferment to complete the film *King Creole,* but refused offers from the marines and the navy to join their branches in exchange for preferential treatment and balked at talk of his serving as a special entertainer for troops. "All I want is to be treated as a regular GI," he said at a press conference. "I want to do my duty and I'm mighty proud to be given the opportunity to serve my country."[32] Whether or not the Colonel had masterminded it, the draft certainly was helping to clean up Elvis's image.

After Elvis had served at Fort Hood, Texas, for approximately six months, tragedy struck. Gladys, at age 46, became ill and on August 14 died of a heart attack. Elvis, who had always been unusually close to his mother, was devastated and did not return to Fort Hood until August 24. Just a few weeks after his return he was shipped off to Bremerhaven, West Germany. Huge crowds and a media circus were on hand for both his departure from New York and his arrival in West Germany, but after that the army banned all fans and reporters from the base. For the next two years, Private Presley quietly served as a jeep driver.

Only one event stands out in these otherwise uneventful years: Elvis met Priscilla Ann Beaulieu, the daughter of an Air Force captain also stationed in Germany. She was 14 and Elvis was 24. They saw one another regularly throughout Elvis's last six months at Bremerhaven.

ELVIS THE ACTOR

Elvis returned from the army in March 1960. Music critic and acclaimed Elvis biographer Peter Guralnick writes that during Elvis's absence the Colonel "had kept Elvis's name in the headlines for the entire two years, a feat that Elvis had never believed possible."[33] In two years' time the worries that Elvis's movements were obscene or that rock and roll caused juvenile delinquency were fading away, and because of this Elvis was able to appeal to an older audience. He reclaimed the spotlight immediately after returning to the United States, quickly recording a record, *Elvis Is Back,* filming *G.I. Blues,* and making his return debut on a television special, *Frank Sinatra's Welcome Home Party for Elvis Presley.* However, Elvis stood still while singing with Sinatra, and the soundtrack for *G.I. Blues* contained mostly ballads.

"Some people were saying Elvis was deserting rock 'n' roll," writes Jerry Hopkins, author of one of the first biographies on Elvis. "No one was contradicting them."[34] Many fans felt—and still feel—that the post-army Elvis was a blander version of his former self; Elvis was certainly never able to recapture that mass hysteria that surrounded him in 1956 and 1957. But rock and roll itself had also changed: The big sellers in 1960 were tame singers like Ricky Nelson,

Fabian, and Bobby Darin. If Elvis was seen less as a rebel it may have been because, as Loyd Grossman comments in *A Social History of Rock Music*, "Rock and roll was becoming more entertainment and abandoning its social and artistic role as interpreter of the world for teenage America."[35] Nevertheless, many fans and biographers agree that, whether because of the Colonel or some other more personal reason, after the army years Elvis tended to put commercial considerations first. "Elvis's career dove straight downward from the day he entered the Army,"[36] writes Marsh.

On March 23, 1961, Elvis gave his last public performance for eight years, a benefit concert aboard the U.S.S. *Arizona* in Hawaii. He continued to record, but throughout the 1960s his music was released on the soundtracks to the movies he starred in. "The King had abdicated his throne,"[37] writes Friedlander.

Elvis starred in a total of 32 films, 25 of them filmed in the years 1961 to 1969. Elvis originally hoped to become a serious actor, but the Colonel and the film studios knew that lighthearted romantic comedies, with a few musical numbers thrown in, would make the most money. Though critics generally agree that the quality of these films grew progressively worse as the decade wore on, all of Elvis's movies were profitable.

Priscilla Beaulieu also moved into Graceland in 1961. She and Elvis essentially lived as man and wife until their marriage in Las Vegas on May 1, 1967. Their daughter, Lisa Marie, was born exactly nine months later.

THE COMEBACK

Eventually Elvis tired of the inane musicals he was cast in. He also began to worry that he was being written off as a has-been. His films were grossing millions, but in 1968 Elvis hadn't had a Top 10 hit since 1965's "Crying in the Chapel." He needed a comeback, and so Elvis and the Colonel met with NBC to arrange a television special. The Colonel wanted it to be a Christmas special, with Elvis singing traditional carols. However, the special's producer and director, Steve Binder, had another idea. Guralnick describes the pitch Binder made: "This was a chance to really say something to the world, he declared to Elvis; this was one of those rare opportunities to do something of genuine consequence; this was Elvis's chance to proclaim, through his music, *who he really was.*"[38] Binder wanted Elvis to revisit his old days at Sun Records, when he had sang what he wanted to simply because he enjoyed it.

For once, Elvis sided against the Colonel, and the result was *The '68 Comeback Special* (it was originally aired with the simple title *Elvis*), a taped performance of Elvis singing his original hits. It was his first onstage performance in eight years, and at the beginning of the show Elvis was noticeably nervous. He quickly rediscovered his love of performing for an audience, though, and when the show aired on December 3 it was a huge success. The images of Elvis dressed in the black leather suit he wore for the special are some of the most memorable of his career.

Elvis followed this up with a string of sold-out performances at the International Hotel in Las Vegas in 1969. These were met with rave reviews from critics across the country. "Elvis is back," the *Los Angeles Herald-Examiner* declared simply. "He had been away."[39] Over the next few years Elvis would return to Las Vegas several times for month-long, sold-out engagements. Audiences at these shows saw a rejuvenated Elvis. He was singing his old hits, and he had also begun wearing his over-the-top jumpsuits and using humor onstage to mock his own larger-than-life status.

THE KING IN DECLINE

For the next couple of years Elvis returned to touring. In 1973 *Elvis: Aloha from Hawaii via Satellite* was aired internationally in an effort to appease his fans around the globe, for Elvis had never performed outside the United States.

But when he wasn't touring, Elvis was becoming increasingly withdrawn, and his personal life was suffering for it. He and Priscilla had been drifting apart, and she finally left him in February 1972. Members of the "Memphis Mafia"—the group of friends and cronies that Elvis surrounded himself with at Graceland—report that he became obsessed with various pursuits, including karate, religion, and his gun collection. Friends also began to worry about Elvis's health. His weight fluctuated wildly: He binged when off tour and then went on crash diets for public appearances. He was also becoming dependent on a variety of types of pills.

While touring, Elvis often used stimulants and sleeping pills to cope with the difficulties of sleeping on the road. Then he added appetite suppressants to help with his weight problems. Eventually he was taking a variety of drugs to help him cope with nausea, headaches, constipation, and depression. After his death, when the facts of Elvis's drug use became public, many fans were shocked to hear that Elvis had been a "junkie." In *The Complete Idiot's Guide to Elvis,* author Frank Coffey cautions against such a rush to judgment:

> Remember—and this is important to understanding Elvis's mentality—these were *prescription* drugs. Doctors had prescribed them for him, so for that reason he probably didn't see an ethical or moral dilemma. And why should he? The drugs were legal! He didn't take them purely for "recreation."[40]

In fact, Elvis rarely drank, and when he met Richard Nixon in 1970 Elvis expressed his concern to the president about the growing problem of teen drug abuse.

But however it came about, by the mid-1970s Elvis was an addict. His unhealthy lifestyle finally took its toll on the night of August 16, 1977. His girlfriend, Ginger Alden, found the forty-two-year-old Elvis unconscious in the bathroom at Graceland. He was rushed to Memphis's Baptist Hospital where, after attempts to revive him failed, he was pronounced dead.

Much has been made of the limited information available about the night Elvis died. Dave McGriff, a deputy attorney general who spent three years investigating the circumstances of Elvis's death, suspects a cover-up: "Elvis Presley was absolutely dead at the scene. . . . Taking him to Baptist for emergency treatment gave the family total control over what happened to the body, and over what information was released to the press. . . . It also allowed them to arrange for a private autopsy,"[41] the results of which were made available only to the family.

TWO VIEWS OF THE ELVIS MYTH

In the years since Elvis's death, fans, the media, and biographers have remembered him in a variety of ways. These portrayals of Elvis generally fall into two categories. First, there are those that focus on the "young Elvis"—the Elvis who sang the blues when no other white singer dared to, the Elvis who bought his mother a pink Cadillac as soon as he made it big, the Elvis who shocked America on *The Ed Sullivan Show.* This is the version of Elvis that is presented at Graceland, which opened to the public as a sort of museum-shrine in 1982.

Then there are those that focus on the "old Elvis"—the Elvis who starred in bad movies, the Elvis who wore ridiculous jumpsuits in Las Vegas, the Elvis who died overweight and addicted to drugs. This view of Elvis was most thoroughly developed by Albert Goldman in his 1981 book *Elvis,* which takes a very condescending approach to its subject.

The best way to understand Elvis, however, is to go beyond these two simplified accounts of Elvis Presley, because, as Marsh notes, they "diminish Elvis by reducing his complexity. . . . Such versions of Presley's story insist that his life was simple and easy to understand. In fact, the life of Elvis Presley was an incredible tangle of irreconcilable contradictions."[42] For example, he was essentially a mama's boy, but was lambasted as a symbol of teen rebellion; he was always humble, yet comfortable with the extraordinary success he achieved; and he was a would-be gospel singer who became the King of Rock and Roll.

This anthology invites readers to explore the many aspects of Elvis's personality and career, as well as the many ways in which he influenced American culture. But his single greatest contribution to American history is unmistakable: Before Elvis, rock and roll was just another musical fad. Ever since, it has been a social force—the voice of young America.

NOTES

1. Patricia Jobe Pierce, *The Ultimate Elvis: Elvis Presley Day by Day.* New York: Simon and Schuster, 1994, p. 15.
2. Jeff Pike, *The Death of Rock 'n' Roll: Untimely Demises, Morbid Preoccupations, and Premature Forecasts of Doom in Pop Music.* Boston: Faber and Faber, 1993, p. 60.
3. Kevin Quain, ed., *The Elvis Reader: Texts and Sources on the King of Rock 'n' Roll.* New York: St. Martin's, 1992, p. 8.
4. Dave Marsh, *Elvis.* New York: Thunder's Mouth, 1982, p. 1.
5. Rupert Matthews, *Elvis: The King of Rock 'n' Roll.* New York: Gramercy, 1998, p. 11.
6. Marsh, *Elvis,* p. 1.
7. Quoted in Peter Guralnick, *Last Train to Memphis: The Rise of Elvis Presley.* Boston: Little, Brown, 1994, p. 29.
8. Quoted in Peter Harry Brown and Pat H. Broeske, *Down at the End of Lonely Street: The Life and Death of Elvis Presley.* New York: Dutton, 1997, p. 15.
9. Quoted in Jerry Hopkins, *Elvis: A Biography.* New York: Simon and Schuster, 1971, p. 22.
10. Quoted in Ernst Jorgensen, *Elvis Presley: A Life in Music: The Complete Recording Sessions.* New York: St. Martin's, 1998, p. 7.

11. Quoted in Marsh, *Elvis*, p. 9.
12. Quoted in Patsy Guy Hammontree, *Elvis Presley: A Bio-Bibliography.* Westport, CT: Greenwood Press, 1985, p. 154.
13. Brown and Boeske, *Down at the End of Lonely Street*, p. 21.
14. Marsh, *Elvis*, p. 16.
15. Hammontree, *Elvis Presley*, p. 155.
16. Pierce, *The Ultimate Elvis*, p. 16.
17. Robert G. Pielke, *You Say You Want a Revolution: Rock Music in American Culture.* Chicago: Nelson-Hall, 1986, pp. 141–42.
18. Pielke, *You Say You Want a Revolution*, p. 141.
19. Quoted in Pielke, *You Say You Want a Revolution*, p. 147.
20. Brown and Boeske, *Down at the End of Lonely Street*, p. 35.
21. Pielke, *You Say You Want a Revolution*, p. 142.
22. Quoted in Paul Friedlander, *Rock and Roll: A Social History.* Boulder, CO: Westview Press, 1996, p. 45.
23. Matthews, *Elvis*, p. 27.
24. Quoted in Brown and Boeske, *Down at the End of Lonely Street*, p. 57.
25. Friedlander, *Rock and Roll*, p. 45.
26. David Rubel, *Elvis Presley: The Rise of Rock and Roll.* Brookfield, CT: Millbrook Press, 1991, p. 59.
27. Marsh, *Elvis*, p. 94.
28. Quoted in David P. Szatmary, *A Time to Rock: A Social History of Rock 'n' Roll.* New York: Schirmer, 1996, p. 53.
29. Quoted in Brown and Boeske, *Down at the End of Lonely Street*, p. 73.
30. Pierce, *The Ultimate Elvis*, p. 15.
31. Pielke, *You Say You Want a Revolution*, pp. 152–53.
32. Quoted in Frank Coffey, *The Complete Idiot's Guide to Elvis.* New York: Alpha Books, 1997, p. 156.
33. Peter Guralnick, *Careless Love: The Unmaking of Elvis Presley.* Boston: Little, Brown, 1999, p. 4.
34. Hopkins, *Elvis*, p. 253.
35. Quoted in Friedlander, *Rock and Roll*, p. 47.
36. Marsh, *Elvis*, p. 135.
37. Friedlander, *Rock and Roll*, p. 47.
38. Guralnick, *Careless Love*, p. 295.
39. Quoted in Brown and Boeske, *Down at the End of Lonely Street*, p. 340.
40. Coffey, *The Complete Idiot's Guide to Elvis*, p. 223.
41. Quoted in Brown and Boeske, *Down at the End of Lonely Street*, p. 417.
42. Marsh, *Elvis*, p. xiv.

CHAPTER 1

Elvis's Early Influences

Tupelo: Above the Highway

Peter Guralnick

Music critic and historian Peter Guralnick describes
Elvis's childhood, from his birth in 1935 through to
his eleventh birthday, when the young musician received his first guitar. Guralnick portrays the Presley
family as poor but hardworking. Elvis was unusually
close to his mother but otherwise appears to have
been a fairly average child. His parents encouraged
his musical ability, which first became apparent at
the age of nine when Elvis entered a children's talent show at the Mississippi-Alabama Fair and Dairy
Show. Guralnick is the author of a comprehensive
biography of Elvis, a two-volume set composed of
Last Train to Memphis: The Rise of Elvis Presley and
Careless Love: The Unmaking of Elvis Presley. The
following essay is excerpted from the first volume.

Vernon Presley was never particularly well regarded in Tupelo. He was a man of few words and little ambition, and
even in the separate municipality of East Tupelo, where he
lived with his family "above the highway," a tiny warren of
houses clustered together on five unpaved streets running off
the Old Saltillo Road, he was seen as something of a vacant if
hardworking soul, good-looking, handsome even, but unlikely ever to go anywhere. East Tupelo itself was separated
by more than just the geographical barrier of two small
creeks, corn and cotton fields, and the Mobile & Ohio and St.
Louis & San Francisco railroad tracks from the life of a parent city which was hailed in the 1938 WPA [Works Progress
Administration] Guide as "perhaps Mississippi's best example of what contemporary commentators call the 'New
South.'" East Tupelo, on the other hand, was a part of the
New South that tended to get glossed over, the home of many
of the "poor white" factory workers and sharecroppers who

could fuel a vision of "industry rising in the midst of agriculture and agricultural customs" so long as the social particulars of that vision were not scrutinized too closely. "Over the years of its existence and even after its merger with Tupelo [in 1946]," wrote a local historian, "East Tupelo had the reputation of being an extremely rough town. Some citizens doubt that it was worse than other small towns, but others declare it to have been the roughest town in North Mississippi. The town had its red light district called 'Goosehollow.' ... By 1940 the tiny community of East Tupelo was known to have at least nine bootleggers."

In 1936 the mayor of East Tupelo was Vernon Presley's uncle, Noah, who lived on Kelly Street above the highway, owned a small grocery store, and drove the school bus. Noah's brother, Jessie, Vernon's father, was relatively comfortable as well, if not as upstanding a member of the community. He owned his own home on Old Saltillo Road, just above Kelly Street, and he worked fairly steadily, even if he had a reputation as a hard drinker and a "rogue." Vernon, by way of contrast, showed little drive or direction. Though he worked hard to maintain a succession of Depression-limited jobs (milkman, sharecropper, WPA laborer), he never really seemed to make a go of it, and he never seemed to particularly care about making a go of it either. Closemouthed, recessive, almost brooding at times, "dry" in the description of his friends, Vernon did appear to care deeply about his little family: his wife, Gladys Smith, whom he married in 1933; his son, Elvis Aron Presley, who was born on January 8, 1935; the twin, Jesse Garon, whom they had lost. He built a home in preparation for the birth, a two-room shotgun shack next to his parents' four-room "big house," with the help of his father and his older brother, Vester (who in September 1935 would marry Gladys' sister Clettes). He took out what amounted to a mortgage of $180 from Orville Bean, on whose dairy farm he and his father occasionally worked, with the property remaining Bean's until the loan was paid off. There was a pump and an outhouse in the back, and although East Tupelo was one of the first beneficiaries of the TVA rural electrification program, the new home was lit with oil lamps when he and Gladys moved in in December 1934.

Gladys Presley, everyone agreed, was the spark of that marriage. Where Vernon was taciturn to the point of sullenness, she was voluble, lively, full of spunk. They had both dropped out of school at an early age, but Gladys—who had grown up on a succession of farms in the area with seven brothers and sisters—took a backseat to no one. When she was twenty, her father died, and she heard of a job at the Tupelo Garment Plant that paid two dollars a day for a twelve-hour workday. There was a bus to pick up the girls who lived out in the country, but not long after starting work she decided to move to town, and she settled herself and her family on Kelly Street in the little community above the highway, in East Tupelo, where her uncles Sims and Gains Mansell already lived and Gains co-pastored the tiny new First Assembly of God Church that had sprung up in a tent on a vacant lot. That was where she met Vernon Presley. She saw him on the street, and then she met him at a typically charismatic, "Holy Roller"–type church service. In June 1933 they ran off with another couple and got married in Pontotoc, Mississippi, where Vernon, still a minor, added five years to his age and claimed to be twenty-two, while Gladys reduced hers by two, to nineteen. They borrowed the three dollars for the license from their friends Marshall and Vona Mae Brown, with whom they moved in for a short time after the marriage.

Gladys had a difficult pregnancy and toward the end had to quit her job at the garment plant. When she came to term, Vernon's mother, Minnie, a midwife named Edna Martin, and one other woman attended her until the midwife called the doctor, sixty-eight-year-old William Robert Hunt. At about four in the morning of January 8, he delivered a baby, stillborn, then thirty-five minutes later another boy. The twins were named Jesse Garon and Elvis Aron, with the rhyming middle names intended to match. Aron (pronounced with a long *a* and the emphasis on the first syllable) was for Vernon's friend Aaron Kennedy, Elvis was Vernon's middle name, and Jesse, of course, was for his father. The dead twin was buried in an unmarked grave in Priceville Cemetery, just below Old Saltillo Road, and was never forgotten either in the legend that accompanied his celebrated younger brother or in family memory. As a child Elvis was said to have frequently visited his brother's grave; as an adult he referred to his twin again and again, reinforced by Gladys' belief that "when one twin died, the one that lived got all the strength of both." Shortly after the birth both mother and child were taken to the hospital, and

Gladys was never able to have another baby. The physician's fifteen-dollar fee was paid by welfare.

Elvis grew up a loved and precious child. He was, everyone agreed, unusually close to his mother. Vernon spoke of it after his son became famous, almost as if it were a source of wonder that anyone could be that close. Throughout her life the son would call her by pet names, they would communicate by baby talk, "she worshiped him," said a neighbor, "from the day he was born." He was attached to his father as well. "When we went swimming, Elvis would have fits if he saw me dive," Vernon recalled. "He was so afraid something would happen to me." And Gladys told of a house fire in East Tupelo, when Vernon ran in and out of the burning building trying to salvage a neighbor's belongings. "Elvis was so sure that his daddy was going to get hurt that he screamed and cried. I had to hold him to keep him from running in after Vernon. I said right sharp, 'Elvis, you just stop that. Your daddy knows what he's doing.'" Elvis' own view of his growing up was more prosaic. "My mama never let me out of her sight. I couldn't go down to the creek with the other kids. Sometimes when I was little, I used to run off. Mama would whip me, and I thought she didn't love me."

In that respect, and in every other, there was not much out of the ordinary about the young Presley family. They were a little peculiar, perhaps, in their insularity, but they were active in church and community, and they had realistic hopes and expectations for their only child. Vernon was, in his own view, a "common laborer," but Gladys was determined that her son would graduate from high school.

In 1937 Gladys' uncle Gains became sole preacher at the Assembly of God Church, which was now housed in a modest wood-framed structure on Adams Street built primarily by Gains. Many in the tiny congregation later recalled a very young Elvis Presley throwing himself into the hymn singing with abandon, and Gladys liked to tell how "when Elvis was just a little fellow, not more than two years old, he would slide down off my lap, run into the aisle and scramble up to the platform. There he would stand looking at the choir and trying to sing with them. He was too little to know the words . . . but he could carry the tune and he would watch their faces and try to do as they did."

It was shortly thereafter that the life of the Presley family was forever changed, or at least diverted from what might have been a more predictable course. Vernon, Gladys' brother Travis, and a man named Lether Gable were charged on November 16, 1937, with "uttering a forged instrument"—altering, and then cashing, a four-dollar check of Orville Bean's made out to Vernon to pay for a hog. On May 25, 1938, Vernon and his two companions were sentenced to three years in Parchman Farm.

In fact, he remained in prison for only eight months, but this was a shaping event in the young family's life. In later years Elvis would often say of his father, "My daddy may seem hard, but you don't know what he's been through," and though it was never a secret, it was always a source of shame. "It was no big disgrace," said Corene Randle Smith, a childhood neighbor. "Everyone realized that Mr. Bean just made an example of him, and that he was on the up-and-up, except maybe that one little time." But it seemed to mark Vernon's view of himself in a more permanent way; it reinforced his mistrust of the world and, while he remained dedicated to his little family, led him to show less and less of himself to others. . . .

Vernon, Travis, and Lether Gable were released from jail on February 6, 1939, in response to a community petition, and a letter from Orville Bean requesting sentence suspension. The Presleys continued to live with Gladys' cousins for a brief time, and all three experienced what Leona Richards called "action nightmares," sleepwalking episodes that none could recall in the morning. They soon moved back to East Tupelo, going from one small rented house to another.

In 1940 Vernon purchased a six-horsepower 1930 Chevrolet truck for $50, and in the fall of 1941 Elvis started school at the seven-hundred-pupil East Tupelo Consolidated (grades 1 through 12), on Lake Street, across Highway 78, about half a mile away from the little village off Old Saltillo Road. Every day Gladys walked Elvis proudly to school, a small towheaded youngster accompanied by his dark-haired, flashing-eyed mother, the two of them clasping hands tightly when they got to the highway, a picture of apprehensive devotion.

"Though we had friends and relatives, including my parents," Vernon recalled, "the three of us formed our own private world." The little boy was as insular in his way as his parents. Apart from family, his few friends from that period have painted him as separate from any crowd—there are no recollections of a "gang," just isolated memories of making cars out of apple crates, playing out behind someone's house, going fishing once in a while with James Ausborn, who lived over by the school. "Mrs. Presley would say to be back at two, and he'd get worried, keep looking at the sun, say, 'I believe it's about two o'clock. We better go.'" He was a gentle boy, his father said; "[one time] I asked him to go

ELVIS'S LOST TWIN

In his book The Inner Elvis, *psychologist Peter Whitmer contends that the stillbirth of Elvis's twin, Jesse, had a profound, lifelong effect on Elvis: As a "twinless twin" Elvis felt driven to prove his uniqueness but also suffered from survivor guilt.*

With Jesse's death, Elvis was left with profound and permanent memory traces formed from his prenatal life with his twin. They could never again be activated in the same way; nor could they ever be removed completely from his consciousness. The resulting dilemma for Elvis was that long before he ever developed the ability to use words to describe what he was experiencing, he knew way down deep that an essential part of him was missing.

He would attempt to fill the void that whole world of amniotic sensory joy left in him. Especially with music—the sounds that once triggered his first sensations of human connectedness—he would try and try again to recapture the basic, primal experience he had once shared with Jesse.

For Elvis Presley, with his twin dead and buried, music could never be just an area of interest, a hobby, or even a gift. It would be more than a driving force within him. Music, quite quickly in the developing Elvis, would go beyond passion to become compulsion. Music, and communicating through music, would define him and shape his relationships, helping some, impairing others. Given his natural talent, music, he sensed, could be his vehicle. It could carry him through to success. It could open a path for him to follow, letting him touch and then possess that bright, shiny star in the night. Music would also prove, in the end, to be hollow and shadowy; it was only half the equation; it could never reproduce the whole boundless galaxy of sensuality and thrill that it had first lavished upon him and Jesse.

Peter Whitmer, *The Inner Elvis: A Psychological Biography of Elvis Aron Presley.* New York: Hyperion, 1996.

hunting with me, but when he answered, 'Daddy, I don't want to kill birds,' I didn't try to persuade him to go against his feelings." Once he learned to read he loved comic books; they captured his imagination—he loved the brightly colored pages and the forceful images of power and success. "Elvis would hear us worrying about our debts, being out of work and sickness," his mother recollected proudly, "and he'd say, 'Don't you worry none, Baby. When I grow up, I'm going to buy you a fine house and pay everything you owe at the grocery store and get two Cadillacs—one for you and Daddy, and one for me.'" "I [just] didn't want him to have to steal one," said Vernon.

For the most part he failed to distinguish himself in any way. At school he was "an average student," "sweet and average," according to his teachers, and he himself rarely spoke of his childhood years, except to note that they had not been easy and, occasionally, to recall moments of rejection. With his father, toward the end of his life, he reminisced about the time Vernon had taken him to see his first movie, "and we couldn't let the church know anything about it." The picture that you see of him with his third-grade class shows a little boy standing apart, arms folded, hair neatly combed, his mouth inverted in that familiar pout. Everyone else—the Farrars, the Harrises, Odell Clark—seems connected somehow, grouped together, smiling, arms around each other's shoulders. Elvis stands apart—not shunned, just apart. . . .

What is not only plausible but clearly the case is that Elvis himself, on his own and without reference to anyone else's dreams, plans, or imaginings, was drawn to music in a way that he couldn't fully express, found a kind of peace in the music, was able to imagine something that he could express only to his mother. Still, it must have come as a surprise even to Gladys when Elvis Presley, her shy, dreamy, oddly playful child, got up and sang in front of an audience of several hundred at the age of ten at the annual Mississippi-Alabama Fair and Dairy Show at the Fairgrounds in the middle of downtown Tupelo.

It came about, evidently (though here, too, the story is unavoidably muddled), after he sang "Old Shep," the Red Foley "weeper" about a boy and his dog, at the morning prayer program at school. His teacher, Mrs. Oleta Grimes, who had moved in two doors down from the Presleys on Old Saltillo

Road in 1936 and was, not entirely coincidentally, the daughter of Orville Bean, was so impressed by his singing that she brought him to the principal, Mr. Cole, who in turn entered the fifth-grader in the radio talent contest sponsored by local station WELO on Children's Day (Wednesday, October 3, 1945) at the fair. All the local schools were let out, teachers and children were transported to town by school bus and then marched from the courthouse lawn down the hill to the Fairgrounds, where they were guests of the fair. A prize was given to the school with the greatest proportional representation, and there were individual prizes in the talent contest, from a $25 war bond down to $2.50 for rides. The five-day-long fair included a livestock show, cattle auctions, mule- and horse-pulling contests, and poultry competition, but the Duke of Paducah and a Grand Ole Opry Company which included Minnie Pearl and Pee Wee King were advertised as well. Annie Presley, Sales' wife, recalled the fair as the highlight of both Presley families' social year, when the two couples would share a baby-sitter and go out together for the fair's last night.

The newspaper did not cover the children's contest or even list the winner of the competition. Over the years there have been a number of claimants to the throne, but to Elvis Presley it mattered little who actually won. "They entered me in a talent show," he said in a 1972 interview. "I wore glasses, no music, and I won, I think it was fifth place in this state talent contest. I got a whipping the same day, my mother whipped me for something—I don't know, [going on] one of the rides. Destroyed my ego completely." Gladys gave a more vivid account in 1956, minus the whipping. "I'll never forget, the man at the gate just took it for granted I was Elvis' big sister and sold me a schoolkid's ticket same as him. Elvis had no way to make music, and the other kids wouldn't accompany him. He just climbed up on a chair so he could reach the microphone and he sang 'Old Shep.'" He probably had his picture taken in the western booth, too, just as he would two years later, complete with cowboy hat, chaps, and western backdrop. Although, somewhat surprisingly, there seems to have been little awareness of his triumph among friends and classmates, and he evidently did not sing at the fair again, Elvis always spoke of the event, without embroidery, as the first time he sang in public, and the whipping is a more convincing detail than the conventional story, which has Vernon listening in on the contest on his delivery-truck radio.

It was not long after the contest that he got his first guitar. The chronology can be argued any way you like (and has been), but it appears likely that he got the guitar for his eleventh birthday, since in all of Elvis' own accounts—and in most of the early publicity accounts as well—he sang unaccompanied at the fair simply because he did not have a guitar. In many of those same accounts he was supposed to have gotten the guitar as a birthday present, and the 1956 *TV Radio Mirror* biography has him getting his first guitar the day after a storm which frightened Gladys and him (the tornado of 1936 had been a traumatic event that literally flattened Tupelo, killing 201 people and injuring more than 1,000). In fact there was a small tornado on January 7, 1946, the day before his eleventh birthday. In any case Elvis wanted a bicycle, he said, and the only reason he ended up with the guitar was because his mother was worried that he might get run over, not to mention the fact that the guitar was considerably less expensive (he got the bicycle not long afterward anyway). "Son, wouldn't you rather have the guitar?" Gladys concluded. "It would help you with your singing, and everyone does enjoy hearing you sing."

His uncle Vester, who played frequently in honky-tonks and at country dances and had a great appreciation for country music, and Gladys' brother Johnny Smith taught him a few chords, but it was the new pastor, twenty-one-year-old Frank Smith, who provided the greatest influence. Smith, who had come to Tupelo from Meridian, Mississippi, for a revival in early 1944 and then returned to stay when he married the Presleys' fifteen-year-old neighbor Corene Randle later that year, distinctly recalled the little boy coming to him with the guitar he had just acquired. "I always played the guitar, and I guess he picked up some from that, because a couple of years [after Smith's arrival] he got a guitar and really applied himself. He bought a book that showed how to place your fingers in position, and I went over to his house a time or two, or he would come to where I was, and I would show him some runs and different chords from what he was learning out of his book. That was all: not enough to say I taught him how to play, but I helped him." From his new-found knowledge Elvis started playing for the "special singing" portion of the service, although Smith had to call him up to get him to perform. "I would have to insist on him [getting up there], he didn't push himself. At the special singings we might have someone do a Blackwood Brothers type of quartet number, different ones in the church would get up or maybe somebody visiting would sing, but there were no other kids to sing with him at that time. He sang quite a few times, and he was liked."

Smith put no particular stock in music other than to glorify the Lord and never found it anything but painful to have to dredge up the memory of teaching an eleven-year-old how to play the guitar when this was scarcely relevant to his life's work. Yet even to him Elvis' commitment to music was clear-cut, not just from his singing in church but from the trips that he, the Smiths, and many other East Tupeloans would make to town on Saturday afternoon to attend the WELO Jamboree, a kind of amateur hour which was broadcast from the courthouse. "A whole crowd went down, grown-ups and kids. You got in line to perform, it was just something to do on Saturday. And he would go to the radio station to play and sing—there was nothing to highlight him, really, he was just one of the kids."

Southern Heritage

John Shelton Reed

John Shelton Reed asserts that, despite his extraordinary musical career, Elvis was in many ways a typical southerner, born into a typical southern white family and raised in a typical southern town. To understand Elvis, Reed maintains, one must realize how racial segregation and widespread poverty combined to make life in the American South prior to World War II very different than it was in the rest of the country. The author examines the many ways in which the experiences of the Presley family reflected larger social trends within the American South. Reed is a professor of sociology at the University of North Carolina at Chapel Hill and the author of several books on southern culture, including *My Tears Spoiled My Aim, and Other Reflections on Southern Culture* and *Kicking Back: Further Dispatches from the South.*

Let me start with an appropriately modest summary of my qualifications for this job:

- Elvis and I have the same birthday.
- I, too, was a teenager in Tennessee.
- My grandparents, like his, were cousins.

Somehow I doubt that you're impressed, and you probably shouldn't be. The part of east Tennessee I come from is closer geographically to New York State than it is to Memphis, more Appalachia than Deep South. My January 8 birthday came a crucial seven years after his: I don't remember the Great Depression, FDR, or much of World War II; and I was just a thirteen-year-old paper boy when Elvis played the Civic Auditorium in Kingsport—too young to go hear him, too young even to want to. Which leaves us only with those grandparents, and I don't know what can be made of that.

A FASCINATING INDIVIDUAL

So I can't speak about Elvis with the kind of authority that impresses southerners. I never even met the man. My knowledge, such as it is, is all second-hand book-learning, not from experience or intuition. And even my book-learning is severely limited. Getting ready for this I checked out what we academic types call "the literature" on Elvis, and I'm here to tell you there's a hunka hunka literature out there. Elvis can't quite match the Civil War (which I'm told has generated an average of a book a day since Appomattox), but since 1968 alone the Library of Congress has catalogued over 300 books about him, in at least nine languages. A magazine-and-journal database includes over 200 articles [since 1990] with the word "Elvis" in the title. You'll find them in publications ranging from the *Journal of Philately* to *Christianity and Crisis, Ladies' Home Journal* to the *UCLA Law Review, Bon Appetit* to *Cultural Studies.* There's an article in *Florists' Review* on how to have an "Elvis wedding," while *Studies in Popular Culture* offers a treatise on "Elvis and the Aesthetics of Post-Modernism." Of course, these databases aren't infallible. One article I turned up had the fascinating title "Surgical Management of Collapsed Elvis in a Jaguar," which sounds like the title of a piece of visionary art. But actually it appeared in the *Journal of the American Veterinary Medical Association* and "Elvis" was just a typo for "Pelvis"—not the first time those two words have been associated. . . .

After all this, I quickly gave up any thoughts I had of mastering what's already been written about Elvis. It probably can't be done. Certainly not if you're going to do anything else. Can anything possibly remain to be said? Clearly the boy has made a name for himself. Long ago Elvis became one of those figures like Scarlett or Sherlock, figures on a first-name basis with the world. (Of course it helped that his first name wasn't, say, Robert.) "Elvis" has even become a common noun, as in one news story I found about a guy known as "the Elvis of Bowling."

How did this happen? The sociology of genius is an interesting study, and every bit as important as the genetics and psychology of it. Elvis had an extraordinary talent, but he also had the great good fortune to be in the right place at the right time for that talent to be recognized and acclaimed. His flower didn't bloom unseen or waste its sweetness very long on the desert air of the First Assembly of God. But whatever the balance of individual genius and social readiness to nurture and to reward it, the combination has clearly made him a figure of unique cultural importance.

HUMBLE BEGINNINGS

So I thought I'd begin with how Elvis was *not* unique—how he was, in many ways, quite ordinary. In most respects, it would interest a sociologist that he was born and raised in an ordinary southern white family, and that he was born and raised in an ordinary southern town. You could even say that the Presleys and Tupelo were extraordinarily ordinary—not just typical but exemplary. The histories of the Presleys and of Tupelo illustrate much broader themes in southern history; one way or another they illustrate important trends from the collapse of cotton tenancy to the rise of Pentecostalism, and implicate high-profile southern institutions from Parchman penitentiary to TVA [the Tennessee Valley Authority, which helped provide electricity in the South].

It's worth emphasizing Elvis's ordinariness, I think, because that's part of his fascination and his appeal. Although he became a remarkable cultural phenomenon, his background and first nineteen years were, in broad outline, much the same as those of hundreds of thousands of other southern white boys. To understand how he was unique, we have to start by understanding how he wasn't. To understand him, you have to understand where he came from. You can't *stop* there, but that's where you have to start.

He was born, of course, in 1935, in Tupelo, the son of Vernon Presley and the former Gladys Smith, and, as Elaine Dundy's genealogical research makes clear, even his ancestry was typical for a southern white boy. Elvis's ancestors, like those of most white southerners, were mostly British. The Smiths, his mother's family, were of English descent, moving west from South Carolina after the Civil War, but most of the rest were Celtic rather than Anglo-Saxon. The Presley name came to America with Scots who settled in North Carolina in the eighteenth century, then moved south and west over the years. Most of Elvis's other ancestors were Scotch-Irish, part of the great wave of migration from Scotland to Ulster to Pennsylvania, then down the Shenandoah Valley to the southern interior from southwest Virginia to Texas.

A FAMILY OF SOUTHERN YEOMEN

The story of Elvis's forebears, like those of many white southerners, was one of restless mobility: settling, then moving on, settling again for a generation or two, then moving on again, escaping problems or seeking opportunity or both, looking for a fresh start somewhere else. Most of them were farmers—after the early 1800s cotton farmers—and most were yeomen of the sort Daniel Hundley described in 1860. "Nearly always poor, at least so far as this world's goods are to be taken into the account," Hundley wrote, their only "inheritance [was] the ability and the will to earn an honest livelihood . . . by the toilsome sweat of their own brows." The southern yeoman wasn't often a slaveholder—he couldn't afford it—but when he was he worked alongside his slaves, and Hundley was amused that he was "not offended when they called him familiarly by his Christian name." . . .

By the beginning of the twentieth century, many of the South's white yeomen had lost their land and had joined the great majority of southern blacks as sharecroppers and tenant farmers. Half the South's farmers—two-thirds of all cotton farmers—didn't own the land they farmed, and half of the South's tenants and sharecroppers were white. Among them were both of Elvis's grandfathers. Vernon Presley's father, J.D., was one of ten children (by unknown fathers) of a "single mother." She supported her family by farming on shares, and her son followed in her footsteps. Gladys Presley's father, Bob Smith, was a sharecropper, too, but soon after he married his first cousin Doll, she went to bed with the tuberculosis that was endemic in the rural South and spent the rest of her surprisingly lengthy life as that classic southern figure, the "shut-in." Bob Smith found it necessary to augment his family's meager farming income by distilling and selling illegal whiskey.

MOVING TO THE CITY

When Vernon Presley and Gladys Smith moved to East Tupelo, they were among the first of their families to leave the land: Gladys to run a sewing machine in the Tupelo Garment Center for $2 a day; Vernon to pursue a string of odd but definitely urban jobs—milkman, cabinetmaker, lumberyard worker, delivery-truck driver (delivering wholesale groceries and also, it appears, bootleg liquor).

Incidentally, Gladys was not unusual in being a working woman. In this century, southern women have actually been more likely than women elsewhere to work outside their homes. Many of them—and probably most of their men— would have preferred it otherwise, but economic circumstances made it necessary. This was certainly true for the Presleys. Whenever the family could afford it, Gladys left the labor force. But they could seldom afford it. She worked for the garment factory before and during her pregnancy. She picked cotton with the young Elvis sitting on her picking sack. She worked at the Mid-South Laundry. After the family moved to Memphis she found work immediately as a seamstress for Fashion Curtains. Later she worked in a cafeteria, then as a nurse's aide.

In moving to Tupelo the Presleys were a small part of a great demographic trend that moved rural southerners into towns, farmers into industrial and service occupations. Vernon and Gladys were only a generation ahead of the Hale County, Alabama, families that were portrayed by James Agee and Walker Evans in *Let Us Now Praise Famous Men.* Those families were still sharecropping when Agee and Evans paid their famous visit in the late 1930s; forty years later their children had made the same transition Vernon and Gladys made: Both men and women were working in service and industrial occupations—welder, meatpacker, nursing-home attendant, and so forth. Economically, they were still near the bottom, but the bottom wasn't nearly so low as it had been in the 1930s.

When Elvis was born, two-thirds of all southerners lived in the countryside and half the South's labor force were farmers; by the time of his death, two-thirds of southerners were urban and suburban folk; fewer than 5 percent were farmers and the sharecropper was an endangered species.

"THE PAST IS A FOREIGN COUNTRY"

What kind of place was Tupelo when the young Presley family lived there? It was very different from the town of today. And it was part of a state and a region that were very different from what *they* are today. An Englishman named L.P. Hartley once wrote, "The past is a foreign country; they do things differently there"—and certainly that's true for the American South. In my experience as a teacher, I've found it almost impossible for young people today really to understand what it meant to live in the South of the 1930s. What it meant to live with the day-to-day constraints and indignities of Jim Crow—not just to live with them, but to take them for granted as simply *how things are*. What it meant to live in a region as poor as the South—a region with a per capita income about the same as that of Venezuela's today, about half of what it was elsewhere in the United States. We need to recognize that those among us who once lived in that South—those who, like the Presleys, grew up in that "foreign country" of the past—made a transition in their lifetimes as dramatic and sometimes as wrenching as emigration.

In 1938 Franklin Roosevelt would describe the entire South as "the Nation's No. 1 economic problem"—this with the Depression going on. A government commission had drawn a picture of poverty, dependence, ignorance, disease, malnutrition, inadequate housing, and environmental degradation that closely parallels accounts of life in the Third World today. The researches of Howard Odum and his colleagues at North Carolina, Charles Johnson at Fisk, and other sociologists of the 1930s provided the basis for that report and showed that the South's problems were concentrated in the old Cotton Belt of the Deep South, that long arc from eastern North Carolina to east Texas where the shadow of the plantation still lingered. In this respect, as in many others, Mississippi was the most southern of the southern states. In 1931 H.L. Mencken had put together indicators of health, literacy, economic well-being, and so forth to show readers of the *American Mercury* that what he called "the level of civilization" was lower in the former Confederate states than anywhere else in the country. And by these measures, Mencken announced, "the worst American state" was Mississippi. . . .

ECONOMIC CONDITIONS IN TUPELO

Tupelo was in many respects a typical Cotton Belt county seat, and to the considerable extent that its prosperity was tied up with the cotton economy, the town was in serious trouble—like the South as a whole. But in some ways the town was unusual, certainly for Mississippi. It had hedged its economic bets, and it pointed the way to the South's future. . . .

Once it had become the junction point for two railroad lines, Tupelo was set to emerge in the twentieth century as a go-getting, industrial town of a sort more common in northern Alabama, Georgia, or the Carolina piedmont than in Mississippi. In 1938 the three-year-old Elvis lived in what the Works Progress Administration (WPA) state guide said was "perhaps Mississippi's best example of what contemporary commentators call the 'New South'—industry rising in the midst of agriculture and agricultural customs." The year Elvis was born, Mississippi elected as its governor Hugh White, who instituted a program he called BAWI—"Balance Agriculture with Industry." Tupelo had been trying for decades, with some success, to do just that.

It's easy to make fun of the kind of relentless New South boosters who could write brochures like this early-twentieth-century one, quoted by Elaine Dundy:

> Wanted! Five thousand enthusiastic, thrifty, loyal people to move to Tupelo and Lee County within the next five years and make this their home. Brilliant opportunities loom for people who come to Lee County which promises to be the greatest and the best county in Mississippi.

A pamphlet from the 1920s called "Tupelo, Premier City of Northeast Mississippi" extolled the city's virtues. Dundy says it was "distributed throughout the South boasting of [the town's] excellent schools, government fish hatchery, Tupelo cotton mills, fertilizer factory, fire and sewage system, its handsome courthouse, its beautiful post office, sixteen passenger trains daily, a beautiful Confederate monument, the annual Mississippi-Alabama State Fair; two railroad systems, a cotton market, a well-organized police station, an ice factory, a creamery, the mills, a hospital, and a Coca-Cola bottling plant." The pamphlet added: "In the city of 6,000, 5,999 are boosters in every sense of the word." And I wouldn't have cared to be the one who wasn't. . . .

Mississippi's combination of economic distress and reliable Democratic voting meant that the New Deal was very much a presence in the state. The WPA provided at least two of Vernon's many jobs: one in the 1930s when he worked briefly on the expansion of the Biloxi shipyard, another during the war when he helped to build "Japtown," a POW camp near Como. Right outside of Tupelo was the Tupelo Homestead Resettlement Project, built by the Federal Resettlement Administration. But the most significant New Deal program for Tupelo was TVA. Thanks to its longtime congressman, John Elliott Rankin, the chief promoter of low-cost power in Congress, Tupelo was named America's "First

TVA City," and when Gladys was seven months' pregnant Franklin Roosevelt came to town, the most exciting event in Lee County since Machine Gun Kelly robbed the bank in 1932. A crowd of 75,000 turned out to greet the president, and thereafter TVA supplied the power for everything from the Carnation condensory to the movie projector at the Strand Theater (which the young Elvis preferred, rats and all, to the Lyric, because it was only a dime). . . .

RACE RELATIONS IN TUPELO

[One] aspect of Tupelo that its boosters didn't emphasize was its pattern of race relations. Day-to-day, the races rubbed along together, but they did it within the usual southern framework of black disenfranchisement, segregation of public facilities and much of private life, petty harassment, and occasionally brutal intimidation. [Historian Vaughan] Grisham recounts, for example, the routine humiliations black Tupeloans experienced at the hands of the police. Many responded by joining the Great Migration that took millions of southern blacks from the rural and small-town South to southern cities and beyond, to the cities of the Northeast and Midwest.

Congressman Rankin may have been a great champion of TVA, but he was better known throughout the nation as a race-baiting southern demagogue. His political career began after World War I when he founded a racist newspaper called *New Era*. Grisham summarizes what that paper was all about: "The favorite themes were the defense of lynchings, pleas for the repudiation of the Fifteenth Amendment and alterations of the Fourteenth Amendment of the Constitution, and general assaults on 'do-good troublemakers.'" Rankin used this platform to get elected to Congress in 1920. A black leader commented later, "Thank God Mr. Rankin got himself sent to Washington or I suppose all of us colored people would have had to leave Tupelo." When Elvis was ten years old his congressman was still running against "interests outside the state who literally hate the white people of the South and want to destroy everything for which we stand."

But it tells us something about Tupelo that Rankin was finally unseated in 1952, when his rhetoric came to be seen as an impediment to industrialization. Although being black in Tupelo was no picnic, the town's boosterism spared it the worst excesses of Jim Crow's death throes. Grisham tells a revealing story. He spoke to a segregationist who had sworn

to kill anyone advocating desegregation, and asked him
about the editor of the *Tupelo Daily Journal,* who had been
a moderate, even liberal, voice in race relations. The man
replied, "I just knew that George McLean [the editor] was a
God-damned Communist, but he was the man who was
bringing jobs into the area and if anything happened to him
we would have all been sunk." All in all, it seems Tupelo was
something of a vest-pocket, Mississippi version of Atlanta,
"the city too busy to hate."

TUPELO'S CHURCHES

So much for the town's economic and political institutions,
and they are certainly much of what made Tupelo Tupelo.
But there were other institutions that were equally important in shaping the life of the town. Although the WPA guide
didn't mention it, Tupelo, like almost every other southern
town, was a city of churches—dozens of them in the town
and the nearby countryside, ranging from the big Baptist
and Methodist establishments downtown to the more modest churches and tabernacles serving the white mill workers
and common folk of East and South Tupelo and the black
residents of Tupelo's three Negro sections. Two Tupelo
churches figure prominently in Elvis's story.

One, of course, is the Assembly of God in East Tupelo,
the church the Presleys attended. It was built by the Reverend
Gains Mansell, Gladys's uncle, and after World War II Vernon himself became a deacon. The denomination was a new
one—founded in Hot Springs, Arkansas, in 1914, it was a
mere twenty years old when Elvis was born—but it was one
of the fastest-growing of the great family of Pentecostal and
Holiness groups that trace their origins to what some have
called the "Third Great Awakening" at the turn of the century. Some of those groups are black, some are white, a few
are strikingly both, but all believe in such gifts of the Holy
Spirit as speaking in tongues; most practice faith healing,
foot washing, and other activities found in scripture; nearly
all have traditions of lively and powerful gospel music; and
none gets much respect from uptown Christians, much less
from secular humanists.

The other Tupelo church that figures in our story is the
Sanctified Church, which met in a permanent tent in the
black neighborhood of Shake Rag. After the Presley's moved
from East Tupelo into town they lived on the edge of Shake

Rag, and much speculation has centered on how much exposure the young Elvis had to the black gospel music being performed down the street from his house. After he moved to Memphis, of course, we don't have to speculate. . . .

ON TO MEMPHIS

When Vernon lost his truck-driving job in 1948, it was time to move on, time for another fresh start, and Memphis must have been an appealing choice. From time to time Vernon had joined the army of southern men who worked essentially as what the Germans call *Gastarbeiter*—guest workers—leaving their families to do factory work in one big city or another. During the war he had worked for a while in Memphis, and he knew his way around.

When the Presleys left Tupelo for the big city, once again they were a typical part of a larger picture. Vaughan Grisham reports that 20 percent of Mississippi's population left the state during the 1950s, the culmination of a movement from the rural and small-town South that was one of the great mass migrations of human history. In 1960 10 million Americans born in the South were living outside the region altogether, mostly in northern cities. We hear a lot about the Great Migration of blacks, but two-thirds of that 10 million were white.

On May 17, 1954, the Supreme Court handed down its historic decision in *Brown v. Board of Education,* a day that came to be known in some white southern circles as "Black Monday." It marked the beginning of the end of Jim Crow, of de jure racial segregation in the South. Seven weeks later to the day, on another Monday, July 5, Elvis recorded a country-flavored version of the rhythm-and-blues hit "That's All Right, Mama," an act of *musical* integration that set the stage for rock and roll. And he knew what he was doing. He said, "The colored folks been singing it and playing it just like I'm doin' now, man, for more years than I know. They played it like that in the shanties and in their juke joints, and nobody paid it no mind 'til I goosed it up." That spring of 1954 Elvis, like the South as a whole, took a big step into the unknown, and neither would ever be the same.

HE DIDN'T GET ABOVE HIS RAISING

I heard a story the other day that reminded me of Elvis. It's about an old boy who was out fishing on one of our power-company lakes in North Carolina when he caught an enormous catfish. He hauled it up on the dock and cut it open, and this genie appeared. "I am the genie of the catfish," it said, "and you can have one wish."

The old boy was startled, but he pulled himself together and looked hard at the genie. "Let me get this straight," he said. "You mean I can have anything I want?"

"That's right," said the genie. "Anything you want."

The fellow looked at his boat, and his dock, and the lake, and scratched his head and said, "I believe I'd like a cold beer."

As I say, that story reminded me of Elvis. Here's a southern boy who had success beyond measure and wealth beyond imagining. He could have had anything he wanted, but, in effect, he looked around, scratched his head, and said, "I believe I'd like a peanut-butter and banana sandwich."

Elvis became a pop-culture icon and—never forget—a phenomenal musical influence. As Bruce Springsteen has said, "It was like he came along and whispered some dream in everybody's ear, and somehow we all dreamed it." Eventually, like all too many other southern musicians, he became the classic hero-victim, doomed by his own excesses. But my point is that he remained to a remarkable extent what he was raised to be in the Tupelo years: a polite and humble gospel-singing southern boy, who loved his mama, greasy food, and hanging out with the boys. As we say in the South, he didn't get above his raising—which is why so many of us who never met him feel as if we've known him all our lives.

Gospel Music

Charles Wolfe

While Elvis clearly was very heavily influenced by both country music and black rhythm and blues, author and Middle Tennessee University English professor Charles Wolfe identifies gospel music as a third major influence in the musician's career. Growing up in the South, Elvis was exposed to both white and black gospel traditions and was particularly interested in a popular white gospel quartet, the Blackwood Brothers. Early in his career Elvis performed gospel standards as a way to improve his image among parents and church groups. Later he hired one of the members of the Blackwood Brothers, as well as other gospel singers, as his backup vocalists.

The few serious attempts to trace the origins of Elvis Presley's music have traditionally focussed on two sources: country music, as exemplified by the honky-tonk and bluegrass styles as they came out of the 1940s, and blues, as represented by the early urban styles of Big Boy Crudup, Howlin' Wolf, and B.B. King. Doubtless these two musical sources can account for much of the very early Presley music, through the Sun years and into the mid-1950s. But for the bulk of Presley's career—through the 1960s and 1970s—these sources can account for only a part of his music. These are the years when Presley outgrew his classification as a rock singer and stepped into the center of mainstream American popular music. His sound and style throughout most of this period is a dense, eclectic complex of a number of influences, and one of the influences I want to explore in this essay is one which has been vaguely acknowledged and talked around for years, but which no one has confronted directly: the influence of white gospel music. . . .

Excerpted from "Presley and the Gospel Tradition," by Charles Wolfe in *Elvis: Images and Fancies*, edited by Jac Tharpe. Reprinted with permission from University Press of Mississippi.

During the late 1940s, when Elvis Presley was growing up in Mississippi, the term *spiritual* was usually applied to black groups and *gospel* reserved pretty much for white groups. The National Academy of Recording Arts and Sciences preserves this distinction in its awarding of the Grammy honors; separate categories exist for Soul Gospel and Traditional Gospel. While it is virtually certain that Presley was exposed to both types of these gospel traditions while growing up, and while it is quite likely that, directly or indirectly, he was influenced by the black tradition, this particular study will deal primarily with the white tradition, an influence Presley often acknowledged.

GOSPEL MUSIC IN MEMPHIS

No one familiar with the history of music in the Memphis area can deny the role of gospel music. The Deep South states of Alabama and Mississippi have always been hotbeds of gospel music activity, ranging all the way from Sacred Harp meetings to the more sedate singing schools of James D. Vaughn and Stamps-Baxter. More than any other Southern city, Memphis became a center and a melting pot for the various gospel styles. This development had little to do with Memphis's alleged reputation as a home of the blues, but was more a reflection of the city's emergence as a media center in the 1920s. By 1923 the city had a powerful radio station, WMC, and by 1927 it was a center for Southern recording activities of major phonograph companies. Many of these records contained important early examples of Southern gospel music, both white and black; in fact, the first white performers to record in Memphis were a group of gospel singers headed by a man named George Long, from Presley's home town of Tupelo, Mississippi. (Their recording was "I'm Going Home to Die No More.") Memphis radio continued to attract gospel music to the area; by the late 1940s the Delmore Brothers and Wayne Rainey were mixing country, gospel, and a blues-cum-boogie sound that captivated the whole Arkansas-Tennessee-Mississippi area. By the time Presley had his first hit record, Memphis had become the site for the annual National Gospel Quartet convention.

Not only was Presley aware of this tradition, but as a young man he intensely wanted to be a part of it. His attention was especially attracted to the group which became the most popular quartet in the Memphis area—indeed, in the nation—in the early 1950s, the Blackwood Brothers. Since they were to form such an important part of Presley's early musical ambitions, it is useful to look at them in more detail.

THE BLACKWOOD BROTHERS

The early career of the Blackwood Brothers is in many ways typical of the process through which many amateur gospel quartets throughout the South became "professionalized" in the 1930s and 1940s. The group was originally a family affair, made up of the sons of sharecroppers from Choctaw County in North Central Mississippi; three young brothers, Roy, James, and Doyle Blackwood, along with Roy's son R.W., began performing in the mid-1930s over station WJDX in Jackson, Mississippi, and over KWKH in Shreveport, Louisiana. They performed in the gospel quartet style that originated with music book publisher James D. Vaughn about 1910; Vaughn found that he could popularize and advertise his songbooks by sending quartets around the country to sing at church gatherings and all-day singings. The original sound of these quartets was not unlike that of some popular barbershop quartets of the day; songs were performed unaccompanied (in most cases), with each singer taking a different harmonic line. In the 1930s Vaughn's major rival in the songbook business was the Texas firm of Stamps-Baxter, and it was V.O. Stamps who heard the Blackwood Brothers and signed them up to be "representatives" of the powerful Stamps-Baxter company.

For a time the group played over KMA in Shenandoah, Iowa, and, after the interruption of World War II and several personnel changes, moved to Memphis in 1950. By this time the group was well established with gospel music fans. While in Shenandoah, they had started their own record company; and in Memphis they expanded this and added a publishing company. Yet their real fame was just beginning. In 1951 they signed a contract with a major label, RCA Victor, and soon had a nationwide hit on their hands, a song called "The Man Upstairs." They also achieved more nationwide fame in 1954 when they won first prize at the Arthur Godfrey Talent Scout Show on CBS. Shortly after the Godfrey show, however, in late June 1954, two members of the quartet were killed in a tragic plane crash in Gulfport, Mississippi. After some soul-searching, the group decided to continue in music, and found replacements for the two members they had lost. One of the new members was a powerful bass singer named J.D. Sumner, who was later to play a major role in Presley's music.

Throughout 1954 and 1955, the years when Presley was beginning his own musical career for Sam Phillips's Memphis-based Sun Record Company, the Blackwoods continued to be the most highly visible and exciting musical group in the Memphis area. By 1954 they were honorary Tennessee Colonels (under Gov. Frank Clement) and the entire quartet was on the staff of Mississippi Governor Coleman, who claimed the Blackwoods as cousins. Compared to the pablum being dished out in the popular music of the day—crooning by Perry Como and innocuous ditties by Patti Page—the Blackwoods' music was lively, fresh, and exciting; and furthermore, young aspiring singers of the time could easily look upon it as the epitome of commercial success and respectability.

ELVIS'S GOSPEL AMBITIONS

There is certainly evidence that Presley did. As a young man in Memphis in 1953 he constantly hung around programs that featured the Blackwoods; on his lunch breaks, Presley would routinely watch the noon radio show over WMPS which featured country artists during the first half, and gospel groups—including the Blackwoods—during the second half. (The show's emcee, Bob Neal, was later to become one of Presley's first managers.) He would also attend concerts by the Blackwood Brothers. Bass singer J.D. Sumner recalls: "I first met him when he was a kid in Memphis living in the projects. In fact, I used to sneak him in the back of Ellis Auditorium so he could see our show." James Blackwood, the leader of the Blackwood Brothers, tells an even more revealing story: "When Elvis was eighteen, when he was driving the truck, my nephew Cecil and three other boys had a gospel quartet they called the Songfellows. They thought one of the boys was gonna leave, and so Elvis auditioned and he would-a joined them in singing around the Memphis area, except the other boy changed his mind. That finished it, and I think Elvis was disappointed, but he still sang with the boys from time to time, during rehearsals. And he often came to our all-night gospel sings at the auditorium."

Cecil later joined the regular Blackwood Brothers quartet, and J.D. Sumner reports that in later years Presley was in fact offered a job with "a major quartet," though he does not specify it as the Blackwood Brothers. "After Elvis started hitting it big in rock 'n' roll, one of the quartets called him back and offered him a job. Elvis went to his father and said, 'Daddy, what am I going to do?' His father said, 'Well, son, you're doing all right the way you're going now, so I would just keep it up.'" The fact that Presley, while starting to change the face of American music with his new rock music, would even seriously consider an invitation to join a major gospel group suggests how much gospel music counted in his musical values at the time. . . .

THE JORDANAIRES

During Elvis Presley's twenty-three-year career on stage, in films, and on records, he continually used established gospel groups among his back-up musicians. Three major groups dominated his back-up music: the Jordanaires (1956–67), the Imperials (1969–71), and J.D. Sumner and the Stamps Quartet (1972–77). In each case, the group came to Presley after establishing a secure name in the gospel field. In each case, the group worked very closely with Presley in developing the texture of the sound that he presented to the public. And in each case, the group found itself to some extent trading off the integrity of its gospel repertoire for increasing popularity in pop music as opposed to country or gospel. . . .

As Presley's career skyrocketed throughout 1956, he developed what would today be called an image problem: across the country, parents' groups and church leaders protested his "spastic gyrations" and "primitive jungle-beat rhythm." Partly to counteract this image, Presley, in his second Sullivan appearance in 1957, sang a slow, almost sedate (even by gospel standards) version of an old country and western standard, "Peace in the Valley," which had been popularized by Red Foley some years before. (Ironically, it is not generally known that the song was in fact composed by black gospel composer Thomas A. Dorsey.) Audience reaction was favorable, and within weeks RCA had rushed out a 45 rpm extended play album containing "Peace in the Valley" and three other gospel standards. The liner notes to the set reflected the attempt to "right" Presley's image by stressing his love for gospel music, but also represented a sincere attempt to reflect Presley's genuine love for the music. Since this was Presley's first attempt to present such music before a wider audience, Calvin Helm's notes are worth quoting:

> To a great many people Elvis Presley has been a surprise. They have been surprised at his style of singing, at his disarming frankness and most of all at his rapid success. To them this album will also be a surprise. But to any of the fortunate folks who have known Elvis, whether as a schoolboy, movie usher, delivery man or performer, PEACE IN THE VALLEY will be no surprise.

> Little older than five was Elvis when he started singing in church in his native deep Southland. Its music was his earliest and he is quick to credit this early and sustained background for its contribution towards his style. In fact, prominent in his personal record collection are most of the records available by the Statesmen Quartet, the Blackwood Brothers Quartet, the Jordanaires and other sacred groups of the South.

> It was, then, no real surprise when on a recent Ed Sullivan TV show Elvis decided to do the title song of this set. Nor were the folks at RCA Victor surprised the very next day when the deluge of wires and letters descended suggesting, requesting and demanding that the selection be recorded by Elvis. This album is the result and it is interesting to note that on these four great sacred numbers Elvis chose to use only the men he normally employs on his popular recording; Scotty Moore on guitar, Bill Black on bass, D.J. Fontana on drums and The Jordanaires. If you are not impressed by the results, I will be surprised.

This was the first real public acknowledgment of Presley's longtime interest in gospel music. . . .

THE IMPERIALS AND J.D. SUMNER

By 1969, when Presley was ready to make his "comeback" and resume touring, the Jordanaires had pretty much completed the transition to pop music and had all the studio and recording work they could handle. Though they continued to record with Presley on occasion, they began to cut down on the tours; Gordon Stoker reported that the group was simply tired of touring and didn't feel up to signing on with Elvis. In their place, Elvis got the Imperials, another group which had been known only in gospel circles; in fact, in 1969, the first year of the Gospel Music Association's prestigious Dove awards, the Imperials won the honors for the Best Gospel Group. Though they had been organized in the mid-1960s, the group was just peaking in popularity (at least among gospel circles) in 1969, the year Presley asked them to join him as a back-up group. . . .

Soon the Imperials tired of the touring circuit, and Presley turned to the man who was to become his closest liaison to the world of gospel music, John Daniel Sumner. Next to the legendary "Big Chief," Wetherington of the Statesmen, J.D. Sumner had the most famous bass voice in gospel music. He had joined the Blackwood Brothers in 1954, after the plane crash had killed the group's original bass singer, and had known Elvis since the earliest Memphis days. It was Sumner who had founded the National Quartet Convention and brought it to Memphis in 1955, and this had made him into one of the leading figures in the commercialization of the gospel music industry. In 1963 he and James Blackwood had purchased the Stamps Quartet Music Company in Dallas, one of the oldest and most prestigious gospel publishing houses, and in 1965 Sumner left the Blackwoods to become manager and singer for the Stamps Quartet. Following the modernizing trend in the industry, the group soon shortened its name to "J.D. Sumner and the Stamps." Shortly thereafter, they joined Presley and remained with him for the last whirlwind years of his career.

In an interview given shortly after Presley's death, Sumner reflected on the longtime attraction gospel music had held for Presley. "No one has ever loved bass singing like Elvis did. He told me one time if he could have his choice he would have been a bass singer. He used to have the Stamps come up to his room and sing gospel music for him and he always joined in singing bass. Elvis did more to change music than anyone. He was raised listening to gospel music and was raised in the Pentecostal church where they have always had great feeling in their music. He got his beat in his music from the Pentecostal church. He took white gospel, black gospel, and country and that was where his music came from."

The Colonel

Rupert Matthews

"The Colonel" was the nickname of Tom Parker, Elvis's flamboyant manager from 1955 until the singer's death. The Colonel exerted an enormous, and sometimes negative, influence on Elvis's career. Parker's primary goal, notes Elvis biographer Rupert Matthews, was to have Elvis make as much money as possible, as quickly as possible. Sometimes this led the Colonel to book Elvis for shows and TV appearances—and later movies—that were lucrative but not necessarily good for Elvis's long-term career. However, in the first years of their partnership, the Colonel played a key role in orchestrating Elvis's rise to stardom. The Colonel's first step, as Rupert describes, was to extricate Elvis from his initial association with Sun Records and instead get him a contract with RCA Victor, a much larger record label.

The partnership between Elvis and Colonel Tom Parker was to be the defining one in the career of the young rock singer; but it was not one which clicked immediately. It took hard work on the part of Colonel Parker, but he was a shrewd operator and set about his task in an efficient manner. It took several months, but eventually Parker became Elvis Presley's sole manager, and came to exert a powerful influence over the progress of the star's career.

THE CARNY

Much has been written about Tom Parker, not all of it complimentary, and he is certainly an enigmatic figure. In part this was because he did his best to hide his true origins, causing odd and bizarre rumours to circulate about him. He was born André Cornelius van Kuijk in Breda, a town in the Netherlands. At some point in the 1920s he visited the United States and returned there in 1929 to join the army as unemployment hit Holland. The 20-year-old van Kuijk served in the 64th Coastal Battery, a unit charged with guarding harbours and coastal towns against shellfire from enemy ships. During the First World War, several British coastal towns had suffered badly at the hands of the German High Seas Fleet. American military planners were determined that the United States would not suffer a similar fate in any future war. As usual, however, the military strategists missed out on the fact that time had moved on, and disregarded the threat of bomb-carrying aircraft.

After three years in the army, van Kuijk married a girl named Mary Ross and took a job with a travelling carnival. His title 'Colonel' has nothing to do with his army service, being an honorary title granted to him by the State of Virginia some years later. By the time he started with the carnival, van Kuijk was calling himself Thomas Andrew Parker and claiming to have been born in Virginia. Although much of this phase of his life is lost in obscurity, one story persists regarding his hit show *Colonel Parker and his Dancing Chickens*. According to this, Parker ran a sideshow in which chickens danced to music from a record player. Although he claimed that the chickens had been specially trained, this was not the truth. In fact the sand in which the chickens danced was laid on a metal plate heated from below by gas flames. The only reason the chickens danced when Parker turned on the music was that he also turned up the gas at the same time.

Whatever the truth of the dancing chickens and other stories, Parker clearly did not waste his time travelling with the carnival. He learned many publicity tricks, and invented others which he eagerly tried out on the punters he attracted to his shows. By the end of the 1930s, Parker had risen from running sideshows to becoming a full-time publicist and promoter. In 1942 he was hired by country music star Eddy Arnold; this was Parker's first taste of the music business and he must have liked it, for he never left it. Having taken Arnold to the top as far as country music was concerned, Parker took on Hank Snow. It was as publicist for Hank Snow's tour that he met Presley.

PARKER COURTS ELVIS

At the time of their meeting, the young singer had a contract with Bob Neal which still had some months to run. It was also clear that Presley and his band owed a great deal to Neal and had no intention of running out on him. However, Parker knew that Neal had his hands full with his various commitments in the music business. He also quickly realized that Elvis was very much a home body, and extremely devoted to his family.

Using his position as tour publicist, Parker began to find reasons for visiting Elvis at home. Whenever he called by, Parker made a point of chatting to Vernon and to Gladys about how well their son was doing on the road. Before long he was emphasizing to Vernon just how much fame and money could come Elvis's way as long as he had the right type of manager. He warned that a young boy needed protection from more predatory executives and the fast women abundant in the music industry. Colonel Parker's argument was helped by the fact that what he said held more than an element of truth. Moreover, he had a good reputation for keeping a close eye on his clients.

Only when he was certain that the Presley parents would accept him did Parker turn to Elvis and to Bob Neal, offering to handle the promotional side of a few concerts Neal had arranged for Elvis and the band. So successful was Parker that, a month later, Presley signed up with him. The contract with Neal still had some time to run, but he seems to have been happy to take a back seat; after all, he was now being paid for doing very little indeed. Parker, for his part, was to take 25 per cent of everything Elvis made. The new deal was set for success. As Parker once told Elvis, 'You stay young and sexy and I'll make us both rich as rajahs.'

FROM SUN RECORDS TO RCA VICTOR

But before Elvis was really able to hit the big time, Colonel Parker had to tie up one other loose end: Sam Phillips and Sun Records. As Phillips would have been the first to admit, his was a local recording company catering for Southern tastes. He had neither the resources nor the contacts to handle a star as big as the Colonel intended Elvis to be. Elvis had to sign with a major record company, and that meant leaving Sun. The Colonel was determined that any major label deal Elvis committed himself to signing would include provision for Sun and Sam Phillips. In the event, all the Sun recordings, whether released or not, were bought out for several thousand dollars, and Sun was allowed to sell its remaining stock for its own profit on the back of new publicity. Sam Phillips accepted the deal and never complained about it after Elvis became a major star.

In fact both Sam Phillips and Bob Neal benefited indirectly from their days with Elvis. As soon as Elvis hit the big time the two men set up Stars Inc., a music management team. Capitalizing on their reputation for having 'found' Elvis, the men attracted a whole stable of young talent, including such great names as Jerry Lee Lewis, Carl Perkins and Roy Orbison.

The Colonel, meanwhile, was putting together a record deal which would be the foundation of Elvis's future greatness. At the time there were three major record labels: RCA Victor, Columbia-CBS and Atlantic. Columbia bid first, offering $15,000. However, it viewed Elvis as a talented country singer and the company was known to have a bias against the rougher end of the rock market. Atlantic made a firm bid next, offering $25,000 up front, but the Colonel was uncertain that the company understood the type of publicity needed.

In the end it was RCA Victor which Colonel Parker accepted. It helped that two stars previously managed by the Colonel were already at RCA Victor. Hank Snow and Eddy Arnold had no complaints about the way they were being treated, nor about the financial deals RCA Victor handled. The deal was finalized on 20 November 1955. RCA paid $25,000, plus a $5,000 cash payment to Elvis himself. It was with this money that Elvis made perhaps his most famous purchase. 'I went out and bought Momma a pink Cadillac.' This perfectly encapsulates every aspect of Elvis's character. He was generous to a fault, devoted to his mother, obsessed with motor cars and instantly drawn to anything flashy—the flashier the better. Although other cars came and went, the pink Crown Victoria Cadillac remained and is still part of the Presley estate.

Elvis's First Major Record

Within weeks, RCA Victor had its new artist in the recording studio. Not only was the technical equipment at RCA's Nashville studio far superior to anything at Sun Records, but the company could afford top quality back-up. In addition to Elvis, Scotty Moore, Bill Black and D.J. Fontana, the company laid on guitarist Chet Atkins, pianist Floyd Cramer and

a trio of backing singers. It took some time for the new ar-
rivals to settle in with those who knew how Elvis worked,
but the end result was well worthwhile.

The first number recorded was *I Got a Woman,* a fast rock
number. Although more than competent, there is, however,
something of the Elvis dynamism missing. Perhaps the musicians were trying so hard to work well together that spontaneity was lost in the process. Two slow songs came next:
I'm Counting on You and *I Was the One.* By the time the
group got to the fourth song they were gelling well together
and the track became perhaps the first and greatest of the
Elvis classics.

Heartbreak Hotel captures the raw energy of the Elvis
sound developed at Sun and on the road in the Southern
states, but with a bigger sound provided by the musicians of
RCA Victor. This was the defining track for Elvis, the moment his skills and energy were honed to a professional
edge which made him the King. For many fans this single
track says it all.

Chet Atkins, later to become a legendary figure in country music, said, 'Elvis was electrifying. He was so different in
everything he did. He dressed differently and moved differently from anybody we had ever seen.' It was Chet who per-
suaded Elvis to record some of the vocals on a concrete
staircase at the back of the RCA Victor studios. The result
was a slight echo which emphasized the loneliness of the
song. It is said that Colonel Parker disliked the 'stairwell
sound', but was overruled and these were the vocals used on
the final record.

Backed by *I Was the One, Heartbreak Hotel* was released
on 27 January 1956. In just over 60 days it was number 1 on
the Billboard Popular Music Chart, the Country Music Chart
and the Rhythm and Blues Chart. No other disc had ever
achieved as much and it marked Elvis as a performer going
places.

A FLASH IN THE PAN?

The day after the single was released, Elvis hit national television. The variety show, the *Tommy and Jimmy Dorsey
Show,* was losing in a ratings war with the *Perry Como
Show,* ironically a major RCA success. In the hope of attracting a younger audience, the veteran Dorsey brothers
sidestepped their big band background to book Presley,

Colonel Parker persuading them to part with $1,250 for that first show. The hoped-for younger audience turned out in strength as soon as it was known that Elvis would be on stage. As usual Elvis made quite an impact with his appearance; knowing black-and-white television would fail to do justice to colour, Elvis appeared in black trousers and shirt with a white tie. When the band started with *Shake, Rattle and Roll,* the teenagers began to cheer, but when Elvis began to dance they went wild.

Jackie Gleason, the producer, at once booked Elvis for five more shows. But even as he signed Presley up, Gleason was telling his colleagues, 'He can't last. I tell you flat. He can't last.' It was a view held by many at the time: rock and roll was a new phenomenon—associated as much with juvenile delinquency and gang fights as with music. Cinemas brave enough to show rock and roll movies had to remove their plush cushions and curtains or risk having them destroyed. Because the musicians involved were, like Elvis, largely young and poor, the music establishment refused to take them seriously and rock and roll was seen by the majority as a violent, unwelcome phenomenon and, hopefully, a flash in the pan.

THE COLONEL'S SHORT-TERM THINKING

To some extent Colonel Tom Parker and Elvis himself shared this view. Elvis did not rate himself too highly as a musician. 'If I stop moving, they'll stop coming,' he said of his fans at about this time. Both he and Parker seem to have considered themselves supremely lucky to have been in the right place at the right time and the Colonel at least was determined to make as much money as possible before the rock and roll bubble burst and Elvis ceased to be fashionable.

It was this short-term view that led to the Colonel making one of his most counterproductive business deals. He set up two music publishing companies called Elvis Presley Music and Gladys Music to produce sheet music for the arrangements and songs made famous by Elvis. The complex contracts these companies had entered into with RCA Victor and songwriters meant that a sizable chunk of the royalties were siphoned off from the songwriters and given to Elvis instead. Many of the established songwriters objected strongly and refused either to write for Elvis or to let him record their songs. Although it gave an instant boost to the Elvis cash flow, the long-term effect was to deprive Elvis of some of the best rock and roll songs of the era.

At the time, however, there were no such doubts. After the Dorsey show, Elvis travelled to New York to record at the main RCA Victor studio. Elvis had his three original backers, but Chet Atkins and the other RCA Nashville stars were missing, replaced by other RCA musicians. Again, the new team got together quickly and established such classics as *Blue Suede Shoes, My Baby Left Me* and *Shake Rattle and Roll.*

Meanwhile, Presley was continuing to play live shows and, on 3 April, returned to television. Again the Colonel booked Presley onto a show which was slipping in its ratings and therefore desperate to obtain a guaranteed audience. The *Milton Berle Show* agreed to pay an unheard of sum of $10,000 for a two-show deal. The first show went out on 3 April 1956 from the USS *Hancock*, Elvis appearing totally in black, apart from a bright pink tie. His set included *Heartbreak Hotel* and *Blue Suede Shoes.* His performance was rather restrained by his own standards, and it was clear the audience was not quite certain how to take it. The few gyrations he worked into the act were greeted with murmurs of disapproval as much as by shouts and cheers.

Three weeks later, Elvis Presley was booked into Las Vegas, the premier live venue for American performers. For once the Colonel had made a bad decision. The Vegas audience was older and more staid than most, with not a teenager in sight. Elvis played for only a week before his contract was broken by mutual consent, the Vegas hotel hired a safe comedian, and Presley went back to his adoring teenage fans.

HITTING THE BIG TIME

The second *Milton Berle Show* on 5 June caused real trouble. As a finale, Elvis performed *Hound Dog,* soon to be released as a single. As the song reached its climax, Elvis grabbed the microphone and undulated around the stage in a manner so fluid, dynamic and overtly sexy that it surpassed anything he had even done on film. There is a brief shot of the television audience where faces register emotions ranging from admiration and wonder in the younger viewers, to surprise and shock in older ones. When Elvis finished, Milton Berle came out to engage the audience in some good natured joshing. He even made a parody of the singer's movements by swinging his hips and shaking his legs. The band cut in with a few bars, and Elvis joined in. But unknown to Elvis or Berle, the damage had been done.

Vast numbers of parents were watching the show to have a look at this Elvis their kids seemed so keen on and they did not like what they saw. Over 700,000 letters of complaint flooded in to Milton Berle. 'Uncle Miltie' had thrown away his reputation for providing wholesome family entertainment. The suggestive movements were too much for Middle America and Elvis was plunged into a sea of controversy. Matters deteriorated when a gas station attendant, in a fracas over what was claimed to be good-natured banter, accused Elvis of punching him. Elvis was eventually cleared, but there was no doubt in anyone's mind that he was the dangerous face of the sinister rock and roll phenomenon.

A few days after the Berle sensation, Elvis appeared on stage at the Sam Houston Coliseum in Houston, Texas. The local newspaper sent along one of its more senior reporters, Dick de Pugh, to see what the fuss was all about.

'The wails and screams of more than 8,000 rock 'n' roll idolizers gave a tumultuous opening to the first show of the famed Tennessee playboy, Elvis Presley, Saturday. The howling "hound dog" artist with the rhythmic accomplices were met with mob hysteria to open their two-performance stand here.

'Presley's appearance was preceded by six variety acts to warm up the crowd into a frenzy. The circus prelude included one torch singer, two acrobatic acts, a comedian, a slack wire act and a quartet. Swept in the [entrance] of the Coliseum by a police guard, the greasy, side-burned hillbilly took to the stage an hour later. Screams and lamentations kept up without relief for four minutes and 50 seconds. He entered the arena like a wild calf and began his bellowing to the tune of his million seller Heartbreak Hotel. *All that was heard of this number was the title. Screams from the crowd drowned out any other sound Presley could produce. Three times he paused his panorama of bump and grind to plead with the audience to listen to him. Deafening roars were the answers each time.*

'In the midst of the teenage tumult, a squad of 50 police officers, emergency corpsmen and firemen were circulating the aisles to keep admirers from rushing the bandstand. Elvis rolled and wiggled through Blue Suede Shoes, *adding his*

hippy oomph to an agonizing rendition of Love Me Tender, *and pulsated vigorously as he groaned though* Long Tall Sally. *Holding his hands to his ears so he could hear himself, he wore a guitar slung around his neck, seldom striking a chord. He rocked on his toes, pointed to the kids in the auditorium and sang to them and made a quick exit on a little number called* Hound Dog.

'Toward the end of Elvis's second show on Saturday night, a hysterical teen-ager with flowing ponytail broke through the police line surrounding the stage and rushed her idol. Police carried her back to her seat, but she had broken the ice. Teen-age girls en masse clamored for Presley, and rushed the stage until the singer was whisked off in a waiting police car to his suite at the Shamrock Hilton Hotel.

'Statistics: No one fainted and no one injured.'

There could be no doubt that Elvis was a major star, with all that that entailed. By the autumn, Colonel Parker was able to joke, 'When I met Elvis he was a kid with a million-dollar talent. Now he's a kid with a million dollars.'

CHAPTER 2

Elvis's Impact on Popular Music

People Who Made History
Elvis Presley

Elvis Mania Sweeps the Nation

David P. Szatmary

David P. Szatmary is the author of *A Time to Rock: A Social History of Rock 'n' Roll*, from which the following essay is excerpted. In it, he explains that while Elvis eventually became known as the King of Rock and Roll, in 1954 he was called the King of Western Bop. The type of music he played, a combination of rhythm and blues and country, was initially called rockabilly. Szatmary writes that in 1954, shortly after the release of his first record, which was an instant success in Memphis, Elvis began playing to crowds of hysterical teenagers throughout the South. Teens outside the South joined the rockabilly craze, and soon Elvis signed with a major record label, began appearing on television, and released several Top 40 radio hits. By 1956, Elvis mania had swept the nation.

Elvis Presley, a kinetic image in white suede shoes, an oversized, white-checkered jacket over a jet-black shirt with an upturned collar, and *no tie.* He violently shook his black zoot-suit pants as he gyrated his hips and legs. A sneering, rebellious expression covered Presley's face, and his greased hair fell over his sweat-drenched forehead. The singer grabbed a microphone as if he were going to wrench it from its metal base and barked, snarled, whimpered, and shouted into it. Elvis warded off screaming fans who pulled at his loose pants, his suit, and his shirt, lusting to tear off a piece of the raw energy that burst forth. Swaggering across the stage, he sang a sexually charged music that fused a white country past with African-American sounds. Elvis Presley, singing to hordes of adoring, frantic teens, delivered a sound called *rockabilly* that would change the direction of popular music.

THE ROCKABILLY SOUND

White teenagers from poor southern backgrounds, growing up in the border states where black and white cultures stood face to face over a seemingly impassable chasm, concocted the pulsating mixture of African-American-inspired rhythm and blues and country and western known as rockabilly. They were teenagers such as Jerry Lee Lewis, who leapt on his piano, banged the keys with his feet, and heaved his jacket, and sometimes his shredded shirt, to the audience; the more subdued Carl Perkins, writer of "Blue Suede Shoes," "Boppin' the Blues," and many other classics; Johnny Cash, who launched his career with "The Ballad of a Teenage Queen," "Get Rhythm," and "Folsom Prison Blues"; Johnny Burnette, the cofounder of the crazed Rock and Roll Trio with brother Dorsey and Paul Burlison; the quiet, bespectacled Texan, Charles ("Buddy") Holly; and, of course, Elvis Presley, the pace setter of the new music, whose raw edge drove crowds to a frenzy. Despite the warnings of many horrified adults, these poor southern whites spread the message of rock-and-roll to millions of clamoring teenage fans and vaulted to the top of the national charts. . . .

These poor youths combined the two indigenous musical forms of the rural American South: the blues and country music. As did the Delmore Brothers in the 1930s and Arthur "Guitar Boogie" Smith in the 1940s, Elvis Presley looked to both African-American and white music for inspiration. A member of the evangelical First Assembly of God Church in Tupelo, Elvis "used to go to these religious singings all the time. There were these singers, perfectly fine singers, but nobody responded to them. Then there was the preachers and they cut up all over the place, jumpin' on the piano, movin' ever' which way. The audience liked 'em. I guess I learned from them."

Elvis listened to such bluesmen of the Mississippi Delta as Big Bill Broonzy, B.B. King, John Lee Hooker, and Chester ("Howlin' Wolf") Burnett, hearing them on late-night radio and in the clubs along Beale Street in Memphis, one of the main thoroughfares of African-American musical culture in the South. According to blues great B.B. King, "I knew Elvis before he was popular. He used to come around and be around us a lot. There was a place we used to go and hang out on Beale Street. People had like pawn shops there and a lot of us used to hang around in certain of these places and this was where I met him."

The Presley sound also was steeped in the country and western tradition of the South—Roy Acuff, Ernest Tubb, Ted Daffan, Bob Wills, and Jimmie Rodgers. In late 1954, Elvis, then called the King of the Western Bop, played the Bel Air Club in Memphis with bassist Bill Black and guitarist Scotty Moore in Doug Poindexter's Starlite Wranglers. At that time, recalled Poindexter, "we were strictly a country band. Elvis worked hard at fitting in, but he sure didn't cause too many riots in them days."

Presley's first recordings revealed his dual influences: a "race" number written by Arthur ("Big Boy") Crudup, "That's All Right, Mama," and a Bill Monroe country tune, "Blue Moon of Kentucky." As Presley indicated at the time, "I love the rhythm and beat of good rock and roll music and I think most people like it too. After all, it's a combination of folk or hillbilly music and gospel singing."

Ironically, at least to self-righteous northerners, southern whites incorporated African-American sounds into their music. "The breakthrough didn't come, as you might expect, in the North," observed Atlantic Record cofounder Ahmet Ertegun. "No, it was 'prejudiced' white Southerners who began programming R & B. They began playing Fats Domino, Ivory Joe Hunter, Roy Milton, Ruth Brown, Amos Milburn, because young white teenagers heard them on those top-of-the-dial stations and began requesting them. What the hell was Elvis listening to when he was growing up?" Added Jerry Wexler, another of the forces behind Atlantic: "Despite the Ku Klux Klan and bloodshed, the Southern white is a helluva lot closer to the Negro psyche and black soul than your liberal white Northerner."

SUN RECORDS AND ELVIS

Many southern rockabillies recorded their brand of raucous black-and-white blues at the Sun Record Company in Memphis, which was owned by Sam Phillips. Phillips, growing up near Florence, Alabama, and working in the cotton fields as a boy, seldom noticed "white people singing a lot when they were chopping cotton, but the odd part about it is I never heard a black man who couldn't sing good. Even off key, it had a spontaneity about it that would grab my ear." He "got turned on to rock and roll immediately, when it was still rhythm and blues," he later related. "I always felt that rhythm and blues had a special viability." During the early 1940s, a young Phillips landed a job as a disc jockey at WLAY in Muscle Shoals, Alabama, moved to WLAC in Nashville, and ended at WREC in Memphis.

"I DON'T SOUND LIKE NOBODY"

In his book Elvis Presley: A Life in Music, *Ernst Jorgensen recalls the legendary story of Elvis's first encounter with Sun Records.*

One day in the summer of 1953, Marion Keisker was sitting at her desk at the Phillips Recording Studio at 706 Union Avenue in Memphis. Out of 706 Union, studio owner and operator Sam Phillips ran a record label called Sun; the Alabama native had opened the facility in 1950, looking to record some of the many African-American players around Memphis and the rich farmland of the Mississippi delta south of the city. What he tapped into was an exploding R&B scene, already one of America's most exciting. The music had become increasingly popular with the fading popularity of big bands after World War II, and all over the area—in Memphis, across the river in West Memphis, Arkansas, and down in Helena, Arkansas, and Clarksdale, Mississippi—black acts were doing good business luring new and exciting sounds out of their rich blues heritage. Sam Phillips recorded B.B. King, Howlin' Wolf, Junior Parker, Joe Hill Louis, and many others at 706 Union. He had even recorded what would later be deemed the first rock 'n' roll record, Jackie Brenston and Ike Turner's "Rocket 88." The little studio also had a service facility where anyone off the street could make a two-sided acetate record for $8.25. There were other, cheaper, less professional places to make recordings around town, places other young musicians used, but Elvis chose Sun. He would later say that he wanted to surprise his mother. Perhaps; more likely, though, what moved him was his burning, unexpressed desire to make music and to become a star.

   Marion Keisker worked for Sam, and with him. She also had her own radio talk show, and a feeling for music. When she asked the nervous, almost unintelligible young man, "What kind of a singer are you?" he responded instantly, "I sing all kinds." "Who do you sound like?" she persisted. "I don't sound like nobody," was his response.

Ernst Jorgensen, *Elvis Presley: A Life in Music.* New York: St. Martin's, 1998.

Phillips, earning certification as a radio engineer through a correspondence program, built his own recording studio in a converted radiator shop on Union Avenue in Memphis to record R & B artists, since, in his words, "there was no place in the South they could go to record, the nearest place where they made so-called race records—which was soon to be called rhythm and blues—was Chicago." He cut sides for such independent companies as Chess and Modern, with such performers as Howlin' Wolf, Big Walter Horton, Joe Hill Louis, Rosco Gordon (who began to combine R & B and country), B.B. King, and Jackie Brenston, who with the Ike Turner band cut "Rocket 88."

The R & B orientation of Sun Records began to change during the early 1950s. Many of the best African-American performers in Memphis, such as B.B. King and Howlin' Wolf, moved to Chicago, the rhythm and blues capital of the world, and the artists remaining at Sun sold only a limited number of discs. Phillips, still in his twenties, also sought a younger audience. As he told *Rolling Stone* magazine, he wanted his records to appeal "most especially to young whites, young blacks and then thirdly to the older blacks. . . . There was just no music for young people then except for a few little kiddy records put out by the major labels." Faced with a declining business in R & B, Phillips confided to his secretary that "if I could find a white man who had the Negro sound and the Negro feel, I could make a billion dollars."

Elvis Presley walked into the Sun Records studio and gave Sam Phillips the sound he sought. In 1953, an 18-year-old Presley recorded the Ink Spots' "My Happiness" as a present for his mother at the Memphis Recording Service, a section of the Sun Studio where anyone could record a 10-inch acetate for four dollars. On a Friday in January 1954, he returned and cut his second disc—a ballad, "Casual Love," and a country tune, "I'll Never Stand in Your Way." Marion Keisker, the secretary at the studio, taped the takes and rushed them to her boss.

After a few weeks, Phillips telephoned Presley to make arrangements for some recording sessions. Presley, guitarist Scotty Moore, and bass player Bill Black struggled without results until finally a disgusted Phillips "went back to the booth. I left the mikes open, and I think that Elvis felt like, 'What the hell do I have to lose? I'm really gonna blow his head off, man.' And they cut down on 'That's All Right, Mama,' and, hell, man, they were just as instinctive as they could be."

Dewey Phillips, WHBQ disc jockey who hosted the R & B radio show "Red Hot and Blue," received the record from the Sun owner the next day. On July 10, 1954, recalled Sam Phillips, Dewey "played that thing, and the phones started ringing. Honey, I'll tell you, all hell broke loose." The disc jockey then interviewed the new local sensation. In Dewey's words, "I asked him where he went to high school and he said Humes. I wanted to get that out, because a lot of people listening thought he was colored." Within ten days, more than 5000 orders streamed into the Sun offices for the record, which hit the top position in the Memphis charts.

ELVIS-INDUCED HYSTERIA

Elvis's live performances began to end in hysteria. "In his first public show," Phillips remembered, "we played him at a little club up here at Summer and Medenhall. I went out there that night and introduced Elvis. Now this was kind of out in the country and way out on the highway, as they say. It was just a joint. Here is a bunch of hard-drinking people, and he ain't necessarily playing rhythm and blues, and he didn't look conventional like they did. He looked a little *greasy,* as they called it then. And the reaction was just *incredible.*"

The mania continued unabated during Elvis's first tour of the South. On July 4, 1955, in DeLeon, Texas, fans shredded Presley's pink shirt—a trademark by now—and tore the shoes from his feet. One female admirer from Amarillo, Texas, suffered a gash in her leg at the concert. "But who cares if it left a scar," she told a *Newsweek* reporter. "I got it trying to see Elvis and I'm proud of it. This must be what memories are made of."

Country singer Bob Luman recalled similar hysteria at Kilgore, Texas. "The cat came out in red pants and a green coat and a pink shirt and socks," he told writer Paul Hemphill, "and he had this sneer on his face and he stood behind the mike for five minutes, I'll bet, before he made a move. Then he hit his guitar a lick, and he broke two strings. So there he was, these two strings dangling, and he hadn't done anything yet, and these high school girls were screaming and fainting and running up to the stage, and then he started to move his hips real slow like he had a thing for his guitar. That was Elvis Presley when he was about nineteen, playing Kilgore, Texas. He made chills run up my back."

Presley, attracting wild-eyed, teenaged fans, began to sell records. In early 1955, the singer had a local hit with "Good Rockin' Tonight." Later that year he appeared regularly on the radio program "Louisiana Hayride" on KWKH in Shreveport, Louisiana, and made his television debut on a local version of "Hayride," which propelled "Baby, Let's Play House" to number ten and "Mystery Train" to the top slot on the national country and western chart. . . .

THE MARKETING OF ELVIS MANIA

RCA Victor lured to its label the performer who became known as the king of rock-and-roll. In 1955, the company offered Sun Records $35,000 for the rights to Elvis Presley's recorded material. Sam Phillips accepted the money and surrendered all of the Presley tapes that Sun had produced. "I looked at everything for how I could take a little extra money and get myself out of a real bind," explained Phillips. "I mean I wasn't broke, but man, it was hand-to-mouth."

In January 1956, RCA began to merchandise Elvis, for the first time using the powerful new medium of television to sell rock-and-roll. Developed during the 1920s, televised images had been offered to the public by the end of the 1930s and after World War II had become much more available. By 1953, 328 stations broadcast to nearly 27 million sets in the United States. Within three years the number of stations had nearly doubled, to 620, and the number of TV sets in American homes had increased to 37 million, showing many programs that previously had been aired on radio. At the time television was dominated by three networks: the American Broadcast Company (ABC), the Columbia Broadcasting System (CBS), and the National Broadcast Company (NBC), the last of which was owned by RCA, the Radio Corporation of America.

RCA immediately slotted the photogenic Elvis for television, booking him for six Saturday night appearances on the Tommy and Jimmy Dorsey "Stage Show," a half-hour variety program hosted by the two big-band leaders. This show preceded Jackie Gleason's "The Honeymooners" and competed with "The Perry Como Hour." After Presley boosted the ratings of "Stage Show," RCA scheduled the singer for "The Milton Berle Show" and "The Steve Allen Show."

In the mid-1950s, RCA used the powerful new medium of television to market Elvis Presley and rock and roll.

By the end of the year Ed Sullivan, who earlier had condemned Presley as "unfit for a family audience," agreed to pay the new rock star $50,000 for three appearances on his show, one of the two most popular television programs in America at the time. Sullivan booked Presley for his first appearance on September 9, 1956. Fearing a backlash from his usual viewers, the television host ordered that Elvis be filmed from the waist up, allowing the teenaged television audience only to imagine the pelvic gyrations that took place off the screen. Creating one of the most legendary moments in television history, Sullivan attracted nearly 54 million viewers, or almost 83 percent of the television audience, to his show and helped lift Presley into national prominence. "Presley is riding high right now with network TV appearances," observed *Billboard,* and RCA's release of "Heartbreak Hotel" "should benefit from all the special plugging."

A week later, the magazine reported that sales of the single had "snowballed," and in a few more weeks it reached the top of the national singles chart.

During the next few months, Presley hit the top of the chart with a number of songs, many of which he had sung on his television appearances: "I Want You, I Need You, I Love You," "Love Me Tender," "Hound Dog," "Don't Be Cruel," and "All Shook Up," the last two written by African-American songwriter Otis Blackwell, who had penned "Great Balls of Fire" for Jerry Lee Lewis. "It was television that made Elvis's success possible," related Steve Allen, who featured the singer on his show. "What his millions of young fans responded to was obviously not his voice but Elvis himself. His face, his body, his hair, his gyrations, his cute, country-boy persona."

Besides television, a new Top 40 format on radio helped promote Presley. It was pioneered in 1954 by radio chain owners Todd Storz and Gordon McLendon to rescue radio from a five-year decline caused by the popularity of television. Top 40 radio involved an instant news concept, disc jockey gags and patter, and a limited play list of roughly 40 hits that disc jockeys spun in a constant rotation.

Top 40 radio, promoting the songs of only a few artists, fueled the meteoric rise of Elvis. "There was a huge change overnight," recalled Russ Solomon, founder of the Tower Records chain. "Everybody was interested [in Presley]. At the same moment, Top Forty radio came into play. As a result there was a very dramatic change in the way you perceived selling records. Your hit titles became more and more important."

THE COLONEL'S EFFORTS TO SELL ELVIS

The marketing acumen of Colonel Thomas Parker contributed to Presley's hit-making success. Born in 1910, Parker got his start in carnivals. Since the circus life, according to the Colonel, "was a day-to-day living," he used his ingenuity to make money. For one of his ploys, he rented a cow pasture adjacent to the circus grounds and during the night herded the cows on the only road through the field, which served as the sole exit from the carnival. When unsuspecting circus-goers reached the exit the next day, they could either walk through ankle-deep manure or pay the Colonel a nickel for a pony ride through it.

By 1955, Parker had abandoned the circus and applied his ingenious techniques to the careers of such country singers as Roy Acuff, Minnie Pearl, Eddy Arnold, and Hank Snow. A year later, remembered one of Elvis's neighbors, the Colonel "in the most polished Machiavellian way" convinced Presley's parents to sign their son to his management company. "Colonel Tom was a salesman, I'll give him that. He sure knew how to sell." Almost immediately the Colonel began to market Elvis Presley to the media. "The Colonel doesn't sell Elvis to the public, dig?" Jon Hartmann, one of Parker's subordinates, later observed. "He sells Elvis to the people who sell to the public, and those are the media people—the television and motion picture personalities, the executives and businessmen who control the networks, the important radio people. It's like an endless trip for the Colonel. Elvis, as a product, always in the state of being sold."

In mid-1956, Hank Saperstein joined Tom Parker in the Presley media blitz. Saperstein had become successful in the advertising industry through his marketing efforts for television creations such as Lassie, Wyatt Earp, Ding Dong School, and the Lone Ranger. Not to be outdone by his competitors, he had even stuffed plastic blowguns in cereal boxes to increase the sales of Kellogg's Cornflakes. Saperstein recognized the "universality" of the Presley appeal and began to plaster Elvis's name and picture on all types of products. By 1957, Saperstein and Parker had saturated the American market.

If a loyal fan so desired, she could put on some Elvis Presley bobby socks, Elvis Presley shoes, skirt, blouse, and sweater, hang an Elvis Presley charm bracelet on one wrist, and with the other hand smear on some Elvis Presley lipstick—either Hound Dog Orange, Heartbreak Hotel Pink, or Tutti Frutti Red. She might put an Elvis Presley handkerchief in her Elvis Presley purse and head for school. Once in the classroom, she could write with her green Elvis Presley pencil, inscribed "Sincerely Yours," and sip an Elvis Presley soft drink between class periods. After school she could change into Elvis Presley bermuda shorts, blue jeans, or toreador pants, write to an Elvis Presley pen pal, or play an Elvis Presley game, and fall asleep in her Elvis Presley pajamas on her Elvis Presley pillow. Her last waking memory of the day could be the Elvis Presley fluorescent portrait that hung on her wall. All told, the fan could buy 78 different Elvis Presley products that grossed about $55 million by December 1957. In addition to 25 percent of Elvis's performance royalties, Colonel Parker received a percentage of the manufacturer's wholesale price on each item.

Elvis and the Birth of Rock and Roll

Patsy Guy Hammontree

In the following essay, Patsy Guy Hammontree posits that in the mid-1950s, a number of trends in American culture had paved the way for the birth of a new kind of music. First, the Tinpan Alley music that had dominated popular music since the 1920s had become stale and predictable. Second, both country and black music were beginning to enter the cultural mainstream. Finally, by the 1950s technology was making records and record players less expensive, so that for the first time young people were becoming a major force in the music industry. These forces gave rise to a new musical trend—what would become rock and roll music. Elvis, a gifted singer and highly charismatic performer, dominated the new musical form. Hammontree is a professor of English at the University of Tennessee.

It is curious to speculate just how history will treat Elvis Presley. Elvis's impact is a result of his passion for perfection as an entertainer, his vulnerability, his self-deprecating humor, and perhaps most of all, his kindness to fans; but those nebulous facets may not get recorded in the Presley chronicle. When the people who were so much affected by him are no longer alive to speak to the strength of his personality, the essence of Elvis may be lost. It is impossible to know if the existing evidence—three television specials along with the two documentaries—will be sufficient to exemplify his extraordinary impact as a personality. Written accounts often fail to give a good sense of his effect on audiences; therefore, if visual mediums fail, history will more than likely evaluate him solely as a singer. Indeed, he can stand as a singer, but social and cultural historians should

not overlook his being much more. Elvis himself never publicly claimed to be a cultural force. For instance, at the 1958
dockside press conference when he shipped out for Germany, Elvis remarked, "I've been very lucky. I happened to
come along at a time in the music business when there was
no trend. I was lucky. The people were looking for something different, and I was lucky. I came along just in time."
This unassuming remark reveals Elvis's perception of himself as an accident of history. The lure of egocentricity was
tempered by his sincere belief that a mysterious metaphys-
ical power made his status possible.

BRINGING NEW LIFE TO POPULAR MUSIC

Whatever he privately thought about his personal success,
he was right in noting that in 1955 there was no musical
trend. The last major shift in music came in the twenties
when jazz made its way into the musical mainstream. Black
musicians had been playing jazz since before the turn of the
century, and gradually white musicians became attracted to
it. Ironically, in the mid-fifties, black music again affected a
change in music. This time, Elvis Presley was the major
transmitter. Rhythm and blues, which was so much a part
of black musical heritage, moved into the white musical
arena. For years, rhythm and blues was labeled "race music." According to some music scholars, however, black music is the only true American folk music; but "hillbilly" music of Appalachia is also American folk music. Either form
is more authentic than the stylized "folk" music of the sixties. Unfortunately for many people folk music has no other
meaning. That is why it has been difficult for the general
listener to recognize that Elvis Presley's "rockabilly"
singing in the mid-fifties was a fusing of two folk music traditions. Bringing new life to popular music, he changed its
direction forever.

From the twenties to the fifties, most American music was
standardized and predictable. World War II, of course, had
an effect on music. Patriotic songs were much in demand
from 1940 through 1945, but on the whole popular music
was romantic and sentimental, as might be expected during
a time of national trauma. Almost as an antidote were novelty songs such as "Marzie Doats and Dozy Doats and Little
Lambs Eat Ivy," "Flat Foot Floozie with a Floy, Floy," and
"Hut Sut Song on the Rillah Rah"; these songs were short

lived, and they created no trend. Pop music consisted essentially of the same type of Tinpan Alley tunes popular since the twenties, clichéd both instrumentally and lyrically. As music scholar Sidney Finkelstein put it, "Music had straightjacket forms and censored inane words." Then hard on the heels of World War II came the Korean War, again placing together servicemen from different regions, engendering cultural development, and affecting musical trends.

THE MINGLING OF REGIONAL CULTURES

The two wars contributed to Elvis Presley's success. From the beginning of World War II in 1941 to the end of the Korean "conflict" in 1953, much of the American population was on the move. Traditionally, this country has a mobile population, but during this twelve-year period, movement was extensive. World War II made jobs at defense plants plentiful, but plants were not equally distributed in all regions. To get jobs, people had to move, particularly Southerners, since almost no heavy industry existed anywhere in the Southeast. Naturally, people took regional cultural patterns with them, gradually integrating what they brought with what was there when they arrived. Military assignments also contributed to change. Young men were stationed in parts of the country and parts of the world they would otherwise never have visited, and they took their musical preferences with them. Further, USO entertainment, designed to satisfy troops from all parts of the country, provided programs with mixed musical genres. Thus, this relocation of people set in motion significant cultural changes, one being the alteration of musical tastes.

As regional cultures intermingled, two distinctly regional types of music, both of which had been generally viewed as lacking in musical style and grace, began to reach the ears of a wider audience. Hillbilly music (now identified as country and western) and "race" music (now identified as rhythm and blues), took on new importance despite their neglect by musical aficionados. As Sidney Finkelstein points out in *How Music Expresses Ideas,* persons influential in dictating musical tastes considered only established European compositions worthy of attention. In Finkelstein's words, "Concert music and opera were predominantly a luxury imported from Europe, patronized by the rich as a plaything in imitation of the European aristocracy, and kept largely for the rich." Other music was considered uncouth. "Pop" music was tolerated; it was, after all, the music of the masses. Jazz had status among certain small elite groups, but rhythm and blues remained unnoticed. Southern mountain music was, on the whole, viewed as quaint but not musically important. The Appalachian poor provided themselves with music since most families had a guitar. Those who could afford radios tuned in to hillbilly stations. Most Southern towns which had stations played plenty of hillbilly music, and there was always Nashville's WSM, a clear channel 50,000 watt station which has broadcast the "Grand Ole Opry" since 1925. Blacks in urban areas—if the city were large enough—could hear their music on stations catering to black audiences. In predominantly rural areas if there was not a city large enough to support a black station, blacks, like Appalachian whites, made their own music, providing the rhythm and blues reservoirs from which ultimately came mainstream rock and roll.

BLACK MUSIC AND WHITE AUDIENCES

Black music, as have other black art forms, has moved slowly into the cultural mainstream. Country music gained national recognition more quickly because it reached a wider audience. Black music reached its audience largely through mail order record companies which exploited the rural Southern market but had no interest in the music or the musicians. Such cavalier attitudes on the part of people processing and distributing the records further hampered the assimilation of black artists into the larger culture. As late as 1950 most white Americans were ignorant of the black sound, their awareness limited to Negro spirituals. Some persons were cognizant of the black origins of jazz and "blues"; rhythm music, however, was essentially a foreign sound to white audiences, and the possibility of its becoming more familiar was greatly limited. Hillbilly music, on the other hand, did have the "Grand Ole Opry," which went out over the powerful WSM, widely disseminating the Appalachian sound. Radio owners and programmers assumed that white Americans did not enjoy black music and advertisers were not eager to sponsor it. Black music was heard primarily on Sundays. Stations often sold or donated time to black church services; but not many whites heard those programs since they were aired in the nonpeak time slots.

With his unique voice and personal appeal, Elvis Presley did more to advance rock and roll than any other musician of his time.

Further, blacks had no recording studios in the South, their nearest outlet being Chicago. Occasionally Chicago-based organizations would transport equipment to the South, Memphis in particular, for limited recording sessions. In the early fifties, an entrepreneur named Sam Phillips organized Sun Records and the Memphis Recording Studio upon seeing the business possibilities in establishing a local recording station for blacks. Ironically, black music recorded at Phillips's studio was not released on the Sun label; it was pressed on other labels.

Much later, Phillips took on legendary status as the man who gave Elvis Presley a chance. Allegedly he wanted to find a white singer who could duplicate the sound of black music, making it palatable to white audiences. His story has become highly romanticized. Supposedly Phillips grew up hearing black music at the knee of a black man who worked for his family in Alabama, and he became attached to black music. Indeed, he no doubt heard much black music, but business more than sentiment was the motivating factor in Phillips's decision to open a recording studio for black artists.

Meantime, a late-night WSM program sponsored by Randy's Record Shop in Gallatin, Tennessee, played some of the first rhythm and blues on traditional white radio. For the early fifties, the program had a liberal sprinkling of "race music." Gradually, the rhythm songs of blacks began to creep into white pop music. Helping the progression was the film *Blackboard Jungle,* released in 1955. Set in a ghetto of New York City, it depicted conflict between a humane white teacher and a group of black and Hispanic students who were suspicious of all whites. The movie soundtrack featured Bill Haley and the Comets, a group of musicians in their late thirties or early forties who had begun to include rhythm and blues numbers in their club acts. One of the film's dominant musical numbers was "Shake, Rattle and Roll," a song already well known to black audiences. As movie background music, it reached the ears of many Americans who never would have heard music either from Randy's Record Shop or from any predominantly black radio station. The rhythmic beat of the song caught on, and it provided an extraordinary boost for black music.

The Growing Influence of Young People

Further, in the mid-fifties, a technological advance facilitated the spread of music in ways not previously possible. Prior to that time, record players were expensive apparatuses. They were often built into a radio console, making them even more costly. The prohibitive price kept them out of range for the average wage earner with a limited amount to spend on entertainment. RCA, in an innovative move, began manufacturing a small record player suited to the new 45 r.p.m. records. Not only was this new record player priced inexpensively, it could also play up to six records at one time, having an automatic device to drop the records. Both the inexpensive records and the reasonably priced record players were now within reach of many who had never before considered the possibility of owning what was essentially a personal phonograph. Young people for the first time could have an influence on the popularity of records.

A MUSICAL WATERSHED

The confluence of these factors meant a musical watershed was inevitable. The highly unlikely figure who emerged to have a phenomenal effect not only on music but other cultural aspects was an unknown—Elvis Presley. With his peculiar style of dress and shrill singing voice (a combination of the falsetto singing of black artists and the whining singing of hillbillies), this young white man with long sideburns and a large, heavily greased pompadour merged the two strains of American folk music—Negro and Appalachian—and gave it a hybrid existence. Elvis was then actually swept along by the swift movement of musical changes. As Glenn Hardin, Elvis's long-time pianist, remarked,

> Elvis was definitely one of the innovators of our time. The music he recorded to start with—that was all wrong to try to start with. People trying to break into the business begin with music that's already accepted and familiar. He didn't do that. He came out with music that was really a new sound to most people. Helping him of course was the fact that he had an exceptional voice that was different from anybody else's. It's a very good voice. It makes a song distinct. I think the turning in music, it would have happened. I don't know when or who would have done it. But it would have happened because music changes every so often. But I don't think it would have been *that* big. There was something about Elvis that made a big—that had a big effect. They'd write after each record, "He's a flash in the pan. He'll never make it." But Elvis had talent. If he hadn't had talent, he couldn't have lasted. People figure it out after a while when a person doesn't have talent. These things don't happen very often. Elvis wasn't exactly first, but he was there when things began to stir a little bit. And he was good.

It is true that Elvis did not single-handedly initiate the movement to a new kind of music, but he did more than any other white musician of the time to advance it. Moreover, in addition to his voice, which attracted many people to him, he had a personal appeal which made his influence stretch beyond his own immediate popularity. He became a cultural curiosity without ever intending to be anything more than a popular singer who had ambitions to someday be an actor.

The King Versus the Beatles: Elvis and the Teen Idols That Followed

Michael Bryan Kelly

After Elvis, the Beatles were the next major musical craze to hit America. Music critics have long debated which of the two had the most impact on the future of rock and roll. In his book *The Beatle Myth,* Michael Bryan Kelly suggests that the impact of the Beatles on American music has been greatly exaggerated. In the portion excerpted below, Kelly writes that Elvis created a new phenomenon in popular music: that of the teen idol, young male musical sensations promoted into enormous popularity by a major record label. Kelly contends that the Beatles, with their "hoody" haircuts and slick management, should be seen as teen idols directly inspired by Elvis, rather than as a new and different phenomenon, as the term "British Invasion" might suggest.

By far the most successful solo hitmaker in the history of rock 'n' roll was Elvis Presley. So it was natural that comparisons between the boy from Memphis and the boys from Liverpool were made back in 1964. The controversy began as soon as the Beatles began their ascent to superstardom in the United States, when kids who loved Elvis began to resent the fact that the attention which had up to then been reserved for Elvis began to be heaped on the Beatles.

When people began to call the Beatles "the Greatest," Elvis fans who had never heard that phrase used about anyone except the King felt threatened. Soon, many magazines

Excerpted from *The Beatle Myth: The British Invasion of American Popular Music, 1956–1969* (Jefferson, NC: McFarland & Co.). Copyright © 1991 by Michael Bryan Kelly.

and radio stations began having reader and listener polls to see which artist was bigger.

THE ROCK 'N' ROLL TEEN IDOL

What was even more interesting to rock 'n' roll fans who liked Elvis and the Beatles was the coattail effects each had on rock 'n' roll. In the wake of Elvis' huge popularity in the 1950s, the rock 'n' roll teen idol was born. All of a sudden, there were lots of good looking, young, slightly hoody male singers who appealed to teenaged, usually female, record buyers.

The classic example of the Elvis-inspired teen idol was the late Ricky Nelson. The story has been told many times about the evening when a girl Ricky was dating swooned over an Elvis record on the radio, and Ricky boasted that he was making a record, too. He had already impersonated Elvis on an episode of his family's television sitcom, "The Adventures of Ozzie and Harriet." Within a week he made his boast come true with a hit record million-seller cover version of Fats Domino's "I'm Walkin'."

Many other teen idols came from slightly different roots. For example, Bobby Vee grew up on country music and liked Elvis. When Bobby Vee recorded his first big hit, "Devil or Angel," his roots would have seemed to be rhythm and blues. Except for one thing—he had never even heard of the Clovers' original R & B version of "Devil or Angel." Bobby Vee got his break filling in for Buddy Holly in concert the day Holly died, and for years sang in a Holly style. In turn, Buddy Holly had been strongly influenced by Elvis, even imitating some of the King's vocal stylings and singing Elvis songs like "Baby, I Don't Care." Much of the Elvis influence on Holly was disguised by the vastly different voices they possessed, but Holly was still a "junior Elvis."

For Holly, Vee and the other teen idols, the situation wasn't so much one of being outright Elvis imitators as it was following a trail Elvis had blazed, and being accepted by the public, either consciously or unconsciously, because of their resemblance to Elvis.

THE ELVIS PHENOMENON REPEATED

When the Beatles took America by storm early in 1964, the Elvis/teen idol phenomenon was repeated, this time in the form of the Beatles/British invasion. The Beatles, like Elvis

The Beatles wave to the thousands of screaming teenagers who showed up to greet them at Kennedy Airport in 1964.

before, blazed a trail for similar artists to follow. Very soon, junior Beatles began to appear, from the Dave Clark Five to Peter and Gordon. Many people thought that it was British music per se that was taking the states by storm. But that was not the case. Solo male British rock 'n' roll superstars like Marty Wilde and Cliff Richard didn't catch on. Hugely popular British female solo singing stars like Cilla Black and Helen Shapiro failed to sell records in the United States. No, it was the junior Beatles, or at least groups perceived as junior Beatles, who were accepted by U.S. teens, much as the junior Elvises had been during the previous decade. . . .

FOLLOWING IN ELVIS'S FOOTSTEPS

If you think about it, the biggest teen idols of all of rock 'n' roll were not Paul Anka or Ricky Nelson, but John, Paul, George, and Ringo. First of all, like all teen idols, they were inspired directly by Elvis Presley. They also had hoody haircuts. Not greaser style, but hoody nonetheless.

If ever management promoted a band into popularity, it was Brian Epstein promoting the Beatles. He moved them from bars and strip joints, and forced them literally to clean up their act. He specifically had them cut and wash their hair. He also insisted that they watch their language and smile a lot. Teen idols were always impeccably dressed. Epstein bought for the Beatles matching collarless suits, boots, and other items of dress which were all the rage in Paris at the time.

After he had the Beatles groomed to his specifications, he literally manufactured their popularity, starting when their first British single failed to make the charts in 1962. Brian bought 10,000 copies himself with his own money, simply to get them on the charts!

When the Beatles' first appearance at the London Palladium flopped, Brian had a photographer take a tight shot of a small group of girls he had asked to scream. Then he sent copies of the photo to all of the papers with a press release claiming that 5,000 screaming girls had swamped the theater.

Musically, Epstein teamed the Beatles with arranger George Martin, who put violins on the Beatles' records and, with songs like "Yesterday" and "Michelle," made them respectable enough to be accepted by parents.

The Beatles' early British hits failed when they were first released in the states in 1963. To give the Beatles a push, Capitol Records' publicists spent an unprecedented sum of $50,000 to promote Beatles music into popularity it could not attain without such promotion. The Beatles got onto the Ed Sullivan show because Epstein agreed to just one-half the fee normally paid by Sullivan to performers. In short, manager Brian Epstein, arranger George Martin, and promoters at Capitol manufactured a teen idol career for the Beatles, collectively turning them from young misfits into teen idols! Had not Epstein ordered John Lennon to never again sing nude on stage (as he did in Hamburg in the early '60s), wearing nothing but a toilet seat hung around his neck, Ed Sullivan (the Beatles' version of Dick Clark) would never have booked them on his "reely big shew!"

None of this discussion is intended as a put-down of the Beatles or the British. Rather, it is to show that rock 'n' rollers are rock 'n' rollers, and that haircuts, clothes, publicity, and swooning girls notwithstanding, teen idol status does not mean that an artist is either untalented or unworthy. It's just part of the package. It's the music "business," after all. . . .

The Beatles no doubt had and still have real talent. But with the promotion, the packaging, the merchandising, the teen music magazines, the posters, and the screaming girls, the Beatles were four male mainstays. Not only that, they often attributed their own early interest in rock 'n' roll to the same guy who inspired all the teen idols—Elvis Presley.

CHAPTER 3

Elvis the Rebel

From the Waist Up: Elvis the Pelvis

Linda Martin and Kerry Segrave

Elvis's music inspired a backlash among adults in the 1950s, who felt that the music contributed to juvenile delinquency. However, what bothered critics most was not Elvis's music as much as it was the way he performed it. Elvis's onstage gyrations were thought to be sexually explicit. Linda Martin and Kerry Segrave, authors of *Anti-Rock: The Opposition to Rock 'n' Roll*, cite critics who decried Elvis's performances as "a strip-tease with clothes on" and "uncomfortably suggestive." Elvis's movements attracted even more outrage after his 1956 nationwide television debut on CBS's *Stage Show,* and in a famous appearance on *The Ed Sullivan Show,* censors ordered that "Elvis the Pelvis" be shot only from the waist up.

"Beware Elvis Presley" warned the magazine *America* in its June 23, 1956 issue. The warning was concerned with his lewd, suggestive, and "downright obscene" stage mannerisms. The magazine felt he might not be too much of a negative influence on young people if he was confined to records "but unfortunately Presley makes personal appearances." Presley started with Sun Records in 1954, went to RCA in 1955, and attained superstardom in 1956. He was the first rocker to attain such lofty heights and his appeal was based largely on his youthful vigor; the sexuality of his stage performances; and his tough guy, Marlon Brando–James Dean image. Bill Haley reached stardom before Elvis but was too overweight, too cherubic, and too old to pose the sort of personal and image threat that Presley carried. Presley's concert performances and TV appearances drew wrath, ire, and indignation from all quarters. It was the TV spots that enabled millions of people of all ages to see Presley for free, at the same time, that speeded up the anti-Elvis attitudes. This very anti-Elvis reaction was also a major impetus to his popularity. Kids figured if he was despised that much by adults he must be worth listening to. This increased popularity in turn fueled more anti-Elvis hysteria.

Bill Haley might have been damned for playing rock and roll, the "bad" music, but Presley, who soon earned the sobriquet "Elvis the Pelvis," was twice damned. Once for doing rock and roll and once for the way he performed it. While the main focus of the anti-rock forces in 1955 had been on the "obscene" lyrics, it shifted away over the following couple of years. One branch led to bans and attempted bans on live rock and roll shows. The second branch was an attack on the performers themselves, and their stage presence.

Song lyrics had been greatly "cleansed" by 1956, particularly by the white artists who were trying to reach a larger mass audience. Those who had attacked lyrics found less to complain about and were forced to zero in on other areas. Performers such as Presley were condemned less for the words they sang and more for the way they sang and delivered those words. Certainly no performer in the early years of rock and roll was subjected to a greater amount of invective and verbal assassination than was Elvis Presley.

"DOWNRIGHT OBSCENE"

Presley would come onstage, spraddle his legs before the microphone, and start shaking both legs at once. He would throw down his arm to pluck his guitar, with his lips curled, or in a sneer, a pained expression on his face. He flailed his legs and then snapped them, knees knocking together while shaking his hips and pelvis. These actions were invariably reported by the newspapers as "bumps and grinds." He also made extensive use of the mike and its stand during his act, straddling it, shaking it, dragging it around the stage, lowering it to the floor and so on. He dressed, onstage, much like the young toughs from the film *Blackboard Jungle*.

At a concert in San Diego, Elvis played to turn-away crowds with what was described as a style that "embraces sensuous gyrations and a savage beat." Nothing untoward happened except the usual loud and emotional response by the crowd of mainly teen females. Yet afterward the San Diego police were moved to warn the singer that if he wanted to appear in their city again he would have to clean up his act and eliminate the "bumps" which were deemed not a fit sight for the eyes of the young and impressionable citizens of that California city. He once performed in Florida in 1955 and the police had forced him to sing without moving.

After he appeared at La Crosse, Wisconsin the local paper branded Presley as "downright obscene" and his performance as nothing more than a "strip-tease with clothes on." Pressure from citizen groups in La Crosse was intense enough that the local company which had booked Elvis, Lyons Associates, promised they would never bring him, or anybody similar, to town again.

A crowd of far less than capacity greeted the singer in St. Paul, Minnesota, which prompted the local paper to address an editorial his way. After denouncing the rocker as no more than a "male burlesque dancer" editor Bill Diehl went on to say he had asked around and discovered the reason for the small attendance, "Moms and dads had seen you on TV and didn't like your unnecessary bumps-and-grind routine." He speculated further that if more parents had seen him the crowd would have been smaller still. Diehl then admonished Presley to "clean it up" if he wanted to prosper in the entertainment business because "nothing grows in dirt."

Since Presley's lyrics were obviously inoffensive, other aspects of his performance were attacked. Compared to the later gyrations of a Jagger or a Morrison, Elvis was relatively stationary. . . .

As [Albert Goldman,] one of Elvis' biographers, has stated, "Elvis was assailed all through his first big year by a chorus of newspaper writers, pulpit preachers, high-school teachers, police officials and local politicians. These folk were . . . quick to identify him as a symptom of the dread problem of juvenile delinquency. Not content just to attack Elvis verbally, some of his assailants demanded that action be taken either to curb Elvis' performances or to run him out of town." This statement does not tell the whole story, for the attacks continued well beyond his first big year and he was seen as a cause of juvenile delinquency by many, not just a symptom. An appearance in Ottawa, Canada resulted in a melee and the next day the press complained that "Elvis provoked the riot." . . .

ELVIS'S TELEVISION DEBUT

Presley made his television debut January 28, 1956 on the Tommy and Jimmy Dorsey half-hour program "Stage Show." The show, on CBS, was produced by Jackie Gleason and preceded his own program, "The Honeymooners." Ratings on "Stage Show" had been low and Gleason had been on a desperate talent search to try and boost the number of viewers when he settled on Presley. When asked about his own opinion of Presley, Gleason has never said more than, "If I booked only the people I like, I'd have nothing but trumpet players on my show."

This TV program marked rock's first, and frontal, attack on the nation's living rooms—and the nation was outraged. [According to Goldman,] the day after Presley appeared "Stage Show" was "flooded with wires, calls and letters denouncing the show and threatening reprisals."

Elvis's next TV appearances were on "The Milton Berle Show" on April 3 and June 5, which provoked the usual reaction. The *San Francisco Chronicle* called his routine in "appalling taste." Jack Gould, TV critic for the *New York Times,* said he had "no discernible singing ability," sang in an "undistinguished whine," and "for the ear he is an utter bore."

Attacking Presley's voice was a particularly inappropriate criticism since the rocker had a good singing voice, better than many of his contemporaries. It only illustrated the ludicrous lengths opponents would go to in order to try and find something objectionable.

Another major New York TV critic was Jack O'Brien who, writing in the *Journal-American,* said, "Elvis Presley wriggled and wiggled with such abdominal gyrations that burlesque bombshell Georgia Sothern really deserves equal time to reply in gyrating kind. . . . He can't sing a lick, makes up for vocal shortcomings with the weirdest and plainly suggestive animation short of an aborigine's mating dance." . . .

It was hoped in some quarters that TV programs would stop handling such "nauseating stuff" as Presley and then he and all his peers could disappear into the "oblivion they deserve." However "The Milton Berle Show" got a huge rating increase on the strength of the Presley appearances and since ratings were the name of the game, other programs, reluctantly or not, picked him up. . . .

"THE ED SULLIVAN SHOW"

That summer Elvis was booked on "The Steve Allen Show" which ran opposite Ed Sullivan's program and was consistently drubbed in the ratings battle between the two. Allen was desperate to boost his ratings, but didn't want the sort of stink that Presley had raised on other programs. Steve Allen's solution was to attempt to stylistically defuse the potential "bomb" that Presley was. Allen had the singer appear in a couple of comic skits and had him sing "Hound Dog" to a real hound dog onstage, without his guitar, without "rocking and rolling," and dressed in formal wear—tie and tails. It was likely the singer's worst and most uncomfortable appearance of his life. Nor were his fans pleased. The next day they picketed NBC studios in New York with signs reading, "We want the real Elvis." The only happy people were Jack Gould who applauded a "much more sedate" Presley and Steve Allen who, for the first time, beat Ed Sullivan in the ratings.

Prior to the appearance on Allen's program Ed Sullivan had refused to book Presley or touch him with the proverbial ten-foot pole. Sullivan had said he "wouldn't consider presenting Presley before a family audience." After being trounced in the rating war by Allen, Sullivan quickly changed his mind and promptly booked Elvis for three shows. Sullivan tried to justify his sudden about face by saying his earlier comments were based just on reports he had heard, but when he actually saw tapes of the singer he said he wondered what all the fuss was about. Nevertheless, when Elvis made his first appearance on September 9, the cameras showed him only from the waist up. A view of the famous pelvis was restricted to those in the studio audience and censored to those at home. That night the Sullivan show captured eighty-two percent of the TV audience.

Jack Gould, the *New York Times* critic, continued to lambast Presley. He called Presley's appearance on the Sullivan show the most unpleasant yet. Deprived of hips and pelvis to fulminate against, the critic assailed the singer because "he injected movements of the tongue and indulged in wordless singing that were singularly distasteful." Even when the hip-shaking was gone this critic stretched credulity to find a physical affront. Gould railed against TV broadcasters for abdicating their responsibility as a public trust by permitting such performances into the living rooms of America. He wanted such displays which "exploited" and "overstimulated" youth to be stopped but he didn't consider the issue as "one of censorship . . . it is one of common sense . . . to ask the broadcaster merely to exercise good sense and display responsibility."

CHARACTER ASSASSINATION

Later that year the singer's agents tried to sell their star to one of the networks in a package of two guest appearances and one special, for a sum of $300,000, but there were no takers. Presley had received $50,000 for his first Sullivan guest spot. An NBC spokesman commented that few sponsors would have the money to afford him and "those that did would be class outfits and most wouldn't want him." *Newsweek* commented on this failure by noting, "The networks showed more taste than Ed Sullivan."

In terms of character assassination and put-downs, few could match these inspired insults hurled at Elvis. A *Time*

PENTECOSTAL GYRATIONS?

Elvis biographer Patsy Guy Hammontree rebuts the widely held view that Elvis's onstage gyrations were "sexually explicit."

Commenting on Elvis's debt to black entertainers, writers Miller and Nowak state, "Sexually explicit movements by a singer had been done before Black audiences . . . but not before mainstream white America." The authors are correct in noting that this kind of movement was unfamiliar to most white Americans, but they are not necessarily accurate in assuming that the gyrations of either Elvis or black singers are intended as sexually explicit movements. Certainly such physical actions can be given sexual shadings, but they are also movements indigenous to certain highly emotional religions in both white and black communities, Pentecostal meetings in particular. In Holiness congregations, gyrations are considered a result of emotional abandon coming from spiritual uplifting. For example, The Dixie Hummingbirds, a black gospel quartet, appeared in 1979 on ABC's "20/20." Their entire program was religious music, yet their movements were almost identical to those gyrations of Elvis when he first began performing.

Patsy Guy Hammontree, *Elvis Presley: A Bio-Bibliography.* Westport, CT: Greenwood, 1985.

magazine review of his first film, "Love Me Tender," read like this:

> Is it a sausage? It is certainly smooth and damp looking, but who ever heard of a 172-lb. sausage 6 ft. tall? Is it a Walt Disney goldfish? It has the same sort of big, soft, beautiful eyes and long, curly lashes, but who ever heard of a goldfish with sideburns? Is it a corpse? The face just hangs there, limp and white with its little drop-seat mouth, rather like Lord Byron in the wax museum. But suddenly the figure comes to life. The lips part, the eyes half close, the clutched guitar begins to undulate back and forth in an uncomfortably suggestive manner. And wham! The mid-section of the body jolts forward to bump and grind and beat out a low-down rhythm that takes its pace from boogie and hillbilly, rock 'n' roll and something known only to Elvis and his Pelvis. As the belly dance gets wilder, a peculiar sound emerges. A rusty foghorn? A voice? Or merely a noise produced, like the voice of a cricket, by the violent stridulation of the legs? Words occasionally can be made out, like raisins in cornmeal mush.

As with most reviews of Presley, the comments were more anatomical than musical. This review encompassed and articulated every conceivable objection to Elvis and illustrated the objections the opposition would find when casting around for something to attack when the lyrics were clean. These ostensible faults were not the real ones—but merely an excuse to attack youth music. . . .

BEYOND THE CRITICS

It seemed that everybody got in on the act, including one used car dealer in Cincinnati who advertised that he would break fifty Presley records in the presence of anybody who bought one of his cars. He sold five cars in one day. In Toronto, Canada a columnist for the *Toronto Telegram* started a club for those who disliked Elvis and rock. It was called the Elvis Suppresley Club. On Canada's west coast, columnist Jack Wasserman of the *Vancouver Sun* held a contest in which listeners were invited to complete, in fifty words or less, the following sentence: "I hate Elvis Presley because . . ." The winner got a Frank Sinatra record album. In the town of Aylmer, Quebec jukebox operators took Presley songs out of the boxes after the mayor-elect urged the ban on the basis that the songs were too suggestive. At a private school in Ottawa, Canada eight female students were expelled after they disobeyed a school edict to stay away from a Presley concert. The principal of the senior high school in Wichita Falls, Texas, Oren T. Freeman, stated that, "We do not tolerate Elvis Presley records at our dances, or blue jeans or ducktail haircuts." The editors of the *Music Journal* blasted Elvis for his "leering, whining, moaning" and for his "filthy performances." Two female students from a San Francisco high school won a "Why I Love Elvis" contest and were flown to Hollywood to be kissed. The principal expelled them and explained, "We don't need that kind of publicity."

While there was at least one critic who felt Presley might not be too negative an influence if he was limited to records, a number of radio stations didn't agree. A jockey known as the Great Scott, in Nashville, burned six hundred Elvis records in a public park. In Wildwood, New Jersey a jockey claimed he couldn't morally justify playing the disks any more and offered to help start a group to "eliminate certain wreck and ruin artists." When radio station WSPT of Minneapolis banned Presley from their airwaves they brought down the ire of some residents. Several DJs reported receiving threatening calls to "play Elvis Presley or else." A rock was thrown through the outlet's front window and the attached note read "I am a teenager—you play Elvis Presley or else we tear up this town." The ban stood. . . .

During his stint in the army from 1958 to 1960 Presley spent parts of 1959 and 1960 stationed in Germany where he aroused just as much of a stir as he did at home. Werner Goetze, a disk jockey in that country, had originally broken the singer's records on the air while describing him as "the whiner." Reaction from his listeners caused Goetze to change his mind and play the records. A German archeologist named Ferdinand Anton was heard on the Armed Forces Radio Network where he branded Elvis as "a throwback to the Stone Age." . . .

THE TAMING OF ELVIS

Little did Presley fans know that the Elvis Presley who emerged from the army in 1960 would bear little resemblance to the Elvis who entered the service in 1958. The change of image was a conscious choice made by his manager, Colonel Tom Parker, who had dominated Elvis in terms of career direction. Presley could have gone into the Special Services branch of the forces and functioned as an entertainer and publicity man. It would have been an easy way to put in his two years; other entertainers had done it. But Parker firmly declined, stating publicly only that Presley didn't want to take the easy way out. Presley served as an ordinary soldier in the army; he was primarily a jeep driver and he received no special treatment. Parker knew that by doing so "the adult acceptance he was picking up would multiply vastly." The army would try from time to time to have Presley perform in some capacity or other during his tour of duty but Parker would always refuse. The colonel was going to make his star acceptable to, and popular with, adults.

It's likely that the tremendous amount of negative reaction to Elvis from 1956 until he entered the army had something to do with Parker's decision to seek adult acceptance. Perhaps no singer before or since has been subjected to such a barrage of invective, bile, and hostile assault as was Presley. The colonel likely feared for the economic viability of his meal ticket a few years down the road if the singer didn't bend to the anti-rock pressures and conform to an image more in keeping with adult expectations.

The first step was to have Elvis serve his time as an ordinary GI. The second was to cancel all live concerts. After emerging from the forces Presley would not do a live concert until 1967, a hiatus of almost a decade. It was the live concerts that had given Presley some of his biggest problems and most hostile attacks. They were difficult affairs since the audience reactions could not be predicted or controlled. A third step was appearance—after leaving the army Presley would not appear again as a greasy hoodlum type.

Presley continued to make TV appearances, but in a more subdued fashion. His first TV show after the army was as a guest on a Frank Sinatra special, one of the most ironic of pairings. Only a scant few years earlier Sinatra had said rock was written, played, and sung by mostly "cretinous goons." But like so many before him Sinatra was desperate. This special was the last of a series of four. The first three had not scored well in the ratings and Sinatra was willing to go to any lengths to prove he could do well on TV. He paid Presley $125,000 for about six minutes of work, a price that galled the older singer. It was agreed that Presley would wear a tux and stand still while he sang. They sang each other's songs that night and joined together in a duet. It was indeed a strange marriage.

A SOFTER IMAGE

Presley's major work after the army was in the recording and film studios. In his records Elvis became more of a balladeer, a crooner of middle-of-the-road pop. His film career saw a softening of his image and the increased use of comedy to give him family appeal. This widening of his appeal, in which Parker was aided by film producer Hal Wallis and the William Morris Agency (Elvis's agents), was all part of a plan "inspired partly by the fear that Elvis's public was too narrow and his stance too controversial; partly by the opportunity, which was offered by his military service, to make a fresh start with a clean, wholesome image."

The tough, hard, and vital rocker named Elvis Presley, who had stirred so much fuss as he helped preside at the birth of rock, would enter the U.S. Army in 1958 and disappear forever. In 1960 a man bearing that name emerged from the army but it couldn't have been the same man. For this namesake was a neat, well-dressed balladeer differing hardly at all from crooners such as Sinatra and Crosby. He was a little younger, that's all. The anti-rock forces had wrought yet another change, wrung another concession from rock and roll.

A Symbol of Teen Rebellion

Peter Wicke

Peter Wicke, a professor at Humboldt University in
Berlin and the author of *Rock Music: Culture, Aesthetics, and Sociology,* describes the 1950s as a time
of cultural conformity. Middle-class teenagers were
under intense pressure to succeed academically and
go on to college, while at the same time the careers
available to those with a college degree were becoming less attractive. Wicke maintains that for many
teenagers, music was one of the main outlets for
their disillusion with the status quo. Elvis was able
to tap into this spirit of unrest because he had
achieved spectacular success without conforming to
societal norms, writes Wicke. And the more the
mainstream media attacked Elvis, the more he became a symbol of teen rebellion.

It was the Eisenhower era, from 1953 to 1960, which shaped
the everyday experiences to which rock'n'roll was linked;
the era of the cold war, a period which saw the conservative
restoration of American capitalism and its seemingly limit-
less economic growth. The Second World War had dragged
the USA out of the depression of the thirties. The victory
over fascist Germany and its Axis partners Italy and Japan
had been an overwhelming one. It had been a just victory,
so that these days we are no longer surprised at the glorifi-
cation of this victory afterwards. The returning war veterans had a right to be feted as national heroes. They now
wanted nothing more than a little peace and to catch up on
what they had missed: earning money, family life, the
dream of prosperity. Against this background their relationship with the ideas of liberalism and bourgeois democracy,
for which they had fought in the war, was bound to become

increasingly uncritical. The result was an anachronistic nationalism which became the dominant ideology. According to David Pichaske: 'What the golden fifties were really about was the unnatural prolongation of World War II heroism and mindset, both of them narrow and atavistically barbarian during the war years, both of them narrow and anachronistically barbarian in the fifties.'

CULTURAL CONFORMITY

This environment was also the breeding-ground for the anti-communist excesses of McCarthyism. In March 1950, in a speech to the American Congress lasting more than five hours, Senator Joseph R. McCarthy had discussed a supposed 'communist infiltration' of the United States. Following this the domestic political climate succumbed to wild hysteria. Julius and Ethel Rosenberg were presented to the now hysterical public as Soviet nuclear spies and, in an unprecedented act of judicial murder, were sent to the electric chair by an American court. The Korean war became the bloodbath of American democracy. Hearings before the Congress committee set up to investigate 'un-American' activities (the House Un-American Activities Committee—HUAC) reached their high point. On the basis of the Loyalty Order more than 2.5 million government employees were subjected to screening. The McCarran Act, which stipulated the registration of communists and communist organisations, legalised comprehensive spying activities by the FBI. The search was not only on for putative signs of 'communist conspiracy'; the snooping also covered drinking and sexual 'aberrations'. In the writer Bernard Malamud's gloomy opinion of this period: 'The country was frightened silly of Alger Hiss and Whittaker Chambers, Communist spies and Congressional committees, flying saucers and fellow travelers, their friends and associates, and those who asked them for a match or the time of day. Intellectuals, scientists, teachers were investigated by numerous committees and if found to be good Americans were asked to sign loyalty oaths.' This explains the cultural emptiness, the social rigidity, the conservatism in post-war America. Conformity became the essential feature of social behaviour.

Because of this, it was teenagers more than any other age group who were confronted at home and at school with a monstrous propaganda campaign for 'American values', for the American way of life. The pressure to conform and to achieve within the American education system grew in proportion to the excesses of McCarthyism and became an essential social experience for this post-war generation. This left its most lasting mark on the high school, the type of school which smoothed the path to social advancement and was a preparation for a college or university education. With slowly rising prosperity in fifties America (at least for the white majority)—the average family income rose by 15 per cent and the average wage by as much as 20 per cent—this became the classic educational course for lower-middle-class teenagers:

> The importance of a college education was inculcated in the mind of every young middle-class American from an early age, partly because Americans have the childish belief that every problem can be solved if only the potential solver has the right credentials and partly because a college education for all one's children was like a barbecue or a new Chrysler, just another suburban status symbol. [Lloyd Grossman, *A Social History of Rock Music*, 1976.]

Thus an increasing number of young Americans worked towards high school entry. Here the fourteen to seventeen year olds were subjected to conventions which nurtured a particular sort of social organism and formed the social background for the rock'n'roll experience. . . .

THE HYPOCRISY OF MAINSTREAM VALUES

The reason why this well-organised educational perfectionism encountered growing resistance at the beginning of the fifties, suffering from a lack of discipline, until ultimately even vulgar, noisy rock'n'roll arrived in its hallowed halls, lay to a not inconsiderable extent in its own nature. The oppressive, claustrophobic atmosphere of conservatism which held sway in the high schools may have suited the political climate of the time, but had for a long time no longer corresponded to the real experiences of the teenagers who were threatened with suffocation in it. The traditional values of a high school education being promoted could simply no longer withstand the social reality. These values were upheld only by hypocrisy. The paradise promised as a reward for successfully completed school examinations and for achieving the best marks proved to be an insipid prosperity which was no longer an adequate goal, because it had become a prosperity founded on credit, a mere facade, unreal through and through. American capitalism, which was radically modernising its methods of production, no longer offered acceptable professional prospects even for those who had completed a higher education. Do-it-yourself capitalism was over and done with. What was required was a host of technical employees who could be deployed at will either to sit out the day in the office or to supervise the automatic production lines; unless, of course, there was the possibility of qualifying for the creative elite of top-ranking scientists in the technological field. This latter was in any case only a prospect for the exceptionally gifted with suitably wealthy parents, for places to study for these qualifications cost astronomical sums because of the necessary expenditure on technical equipment. The lack of a common purpose in life therefore became the basic experience of this generation. . . .

THE INNER CONFLICT THAT ROCK'N'ROLL REPRESENTS

The conservatism of country music on the one hand and the rebellious energy of rhythm & blues on the other became the essence of rock'n'roll, revealing an ambivalence which exactly suited the way high school teenagers felt about life. Wanting to do everything differently from their parents and yet wanting to be exactly the same, seeing prosperity and consumption as the essential conditions of a meaningful life, but no longer believing in such a life; this was the nature of the inner conflict with which this generation of teenagers struggled. Rock'n'roll reduced this to a musical formula, expressing both the noisy rebellion and the secret conformity. Thus, it could become the medium which was able to grasp, to absorb and to pass on the contradictory experiences of teenagers.

The first explicit expression of this inner conflict was in the recordings made for the small Sun label of the Memphis Recording Service in July 1954 by a young man completely unknown at the time, a truck driver with Crown Electric Company—Elvis Presley. The Memphis Recording Service was one of those one-man companies hoping at some point to strike gold in the music market. One of its sources of income, apart from recordings of the unknown blues singers of the region which it then sold on to the large record companies, was a record making service for anyone who wanted to use it. For just a few dollars anyone could go into the studio and have a record made for his own private use. When Elvis Presley first tried out his singing skills here at his own expense in the summer of 1953, he had just left Humes High School in Memphis and, faced with rather modest results in his final examinations, had nothing more in mind than a job as a driver. Up to this point his development had in many ways been typical of the teenagers of his generation in small-town America. Born in 1935 in Tulepo, Mississippi into an impoverished lower-middle-class family—his father had been a self-employed truck driver before working for a trucking firm—and growing up in Memphis where he finally succeeded in entering high school, he had direct experience of the dreary everyday reality of lower-middle-class life and of the overwhelming conformity of the time. Elvis' reaction was indifference and a deep reluctance to accept any responsibility which might have forced him to submit to the constraints of being a proper young man, which was what high school had tried to make of him and his contemporaries. His first encounter with music dated back to his pre-school days and the church choir of the Pentecostal First Assembly of God church in Memphis. At the age of ten he won a prize in a school singing competition at the Mississippi-Alabama Fair and Dairy Show. He played the guitar a little—his parents had given him a guitar for his eleventh birthday—listened to the radio for hours on end and, like all his contemporaries, developed a preference for the earthiness of rhythm & blues and the rough ballads of country music. In this respect his home city of Memphis offered a fascinating spectrum of the South's musical traditions. There was an independent local blues development, dating back to the early twenties, a distinctive gospel tradition in the black churches and an extensive selection of country music in the boorish hillbilly style. Memphis had the first black-run radio station in the USA and famous blues musicians like Howlin' Wolf and Sonny Boy Williamson had their own programmes on the local radio.

ELVIS' APPEAL TO TEENAGERS

In the summer of 1954 the Memphis Recording Service finally gave in to Presley's insistence and produced a commercial record with him. Like all the following five singles on the in-house Sun label it consisted simply of a selection from this musical spectrum, oriented towards the musical tastes of his former high school classmates. 'That's All Right

Teenage girls use lipstick to add their names to the bottom of an Elvis Presley movie poster.

(Mama)' by the blues singer Arthur Big Boy Crudup on the A side was coupled with 'Blue Moon of Kentucky', which Bill Monroe had made a country music classic. This combination matched the mood of the time exactly, especially since Presley sang both songs completely unpretentiously with the spontaneity of the amateur, quite unconcerned about their original stylistic characteristics. 'That's All Right', for example, is unsophisticated conventional blues, easy to sing and simple in style. Presley's voice—with its rather nasal tone far removed from the sensuous expressiveness of Afro-American blues singing—together with the rhythm guitar marking the beat by strumming chords, with the crude bass moving in simple tone steps and the melody guitar supporting the singer, gave this song an absolutely unmistakable character, which sought to make up for its obvious clumsiness with an almost movingly comic enthusiasm. Nothing seemed to go together properly: the voice did not suit the conventional style of the song, the country-style strumming of the rhythm guitar did not suit the blues-style melody guitar, and the unbridled enthusiasm did not suit the banality of the lyrics. But it was precisely these factors which gave the song as a whole its irrepressible image of rebellion. Teenagers felt the singer was one of them. He was someone who had succeeded and with his unprofessional musicality had really shown the others, the adults, what teenagers could achieve. No, they were not failures simply because they tried to reject the conformity, the norms, the rules and the discipline of high school or at best bowed to them with a show of reluctance. They just wanted to be *different*, admittedly without quite knowing *how*; but basically they were not questioning the rules of the society they lived in. To them Elvis Presley was significant because, representing them all, he had succeeded in penetrating a particular social sphere—the music business—and making himself respected there without accepting its norms. This was quite clear in his records, in their naive dilettantism, measured against the professional standards of the time, and in the provocative impudence with which they displayed this naivety. Paul Willis' opinion [in his book *Profane Culture*] is very accurate.

> The assertive masculinity of the motor-bike boys also found an answering structure in their preferred music. Elvis Presley's records were full of aggression. Though the focus was often unspecified and enigmatic, the charge of feeling was strong. In the atmosphere of the music, in the words, in the articulation of the words, in his personal image, was a deep implication that here was a man not to be pushed around. His whole presence demanded that he should be given respect, though, by conventional standards, the grounds for that respect were disreputable and anti-social.

Elvis Presley embodied the uncertain and consuming desire of American high school teenagers in the fifties, the desire somehow to escape the oppressive ordinariness which surrounded them without having to pay the bitter price of conformity. His quick success seemed to be the proof that, in principle, escape was possible. Even though his songs were simply cover versions of songs which had been around for a long time—and not a few songs in Elvis Presley's repertoire belonged in this category—they thus acquired an additional dimension. Presley finally made these songs 'their' music, for he was one of them. It was no longer an alien cultural identity which spoke through these songs, the identity of outlaws, of the Afro-American and white 'fringe groups' from the lower end of the social scale, but their own. Teen-agers had integrated this music into the context of their lifestyle, accompanied by the derogatory remarks of adults, threatened by parental bans and school disciplinary mea-sures. Through Elvis Presley this context was now public, sanctioned by the music business. The whole commercial fuss about him was their social justification. The effect of this was overwhelming. The country singer Bob Luman later described the effect Elvis had at a time when, shortly after the release of his first single, he was still going from one Southern high school ball to another:

> This cat came out in red pants and a green coat and a pink shirt and socks, and he had this sneer on his face and he stood behind the mike for five minutes, I'll bet, before he made a move. Then he hit his guitar a lick, and he broke two strings. I'd been playing ten years, and I hadn't broken a *total* of two strings. So there he was, these two strings dangling, and he hadn't done anything yet, and these high school girls were screaming and fainting and running up to the stage, and then he started to move his hips real slow like he had a thing for his guitar. That was Elvis Presley when he was about 19, playing Kilgore, Texas.

ELVIS' SOCIAL POWER

What Bob Luman was describing was not at all the mystical effect of a charismatic personality, which was how the music industry tried to promote Elvis; neither was it the supposed 'ecstatic' effect of rock music, an effect attributed to rock be-cause of these sorts of scenes. It was far more a reaction to the social phenomenon of Elvis Presley, to the mere fact of his existence in the musty conservative atmosphere of the Eisenhower era. And the more the media turned this reaction into an anti-American threat, the more it gained in strength. In the fact that, with Elvis Presley, for the first time one of them was on stage—someone the same age as them, with the same experiences and someone who was precisely as outra-geous and provocative as they would at least have liked to be—his young audience experienced its social power. And the more the media blew this up into an attack on America, the more colossal this power seemed. [According to writer Mathias R. Schmidt,] 'Reactionaries and patriots saw in the demonstrably rebellious music cult a malicious attempt by the communists to undermine American society through its young people.' The public anti-rock'n'roll campaigns in America, stirred up and accompanied by internal arguments in the music industry—the Broadway publishing empires correctly foresaw the danger to their existence which the victorious progress of rock'n'roll represented—could only hide for a short time the fact that Elvis Presley and rock'n'roll did not stand for a rejection of the American way of life. They stood for a different, more up-to-date and less conservative version, a version which American capitalism itself had ultimately given birth to. [Music critic] Greil Marcus wrote later: 'The version of the American dream that is Elvis' performance is blown up again and again, to contain more history, more people, more music, more hopes; the air gets thin but the bubble does not burst, nor will it ever. This is America when it has outstripped itself, in all of its extravagance.'

Elvis and Race Relations: Blurring the Line Between Black and White

Leonard Pitts Jr.

Leonard Pitts Jr., a columnist for the *Miami Herald,* believes that Elvis's greatest contribution to American society was his effect on race relations. Elvis came along in the fiercest years of racial segregation, he writes, and played a key role in ending it. By combining country with rhythm and blues (R&B), Elvis's music embodied the (at the time) revolutionary idea that black culture and white culture could be brought together. The influence of black culture on Elvis's music is evidenced by the fact that he was consistently at the top of *Billboard* magazine's R&B charts. Elvis's popularity forced mainstream white America to acknowledge black culture, and in the 1950s, maintains Pitts, this was nothing short of a miracle.

Twenty years ago [August 1977], Elvis Presley died and I didn't care.

It wasn't antipathy I felt, but ambivalence. In those days I was associate editor of *SOUL* ("America's Most Soulful Newsmagazine"), a tabloid covering black entertainment. As far as I was concerned, Presley's death had nothing to do with me or my readers; he was irrelevant.

Nor was I alone in that estimation. Indeed I was, at 19, part of that post–Civil Rights school of black thought whose rejection of Elvis was pure reflex. We had a sense that Elvis Presley was an interloper who raided black culture and exploited it to a degree that blacks, being black, never could. It

Reprinted from "In His Life and Music, Elvis Exposed the Lie Behind Segregation," by Leonard Pitts Jr., Knight-Ridder/Tribune News Service, August 11, 1997. Reprinted with permission from Knight-Ridder/Tribune News Service.

was like being made to live on the back porch of your own
house and it raised a mighty resentment. Calling Presley the
King of Rock 'n' Roll was, we felt, not unlike calling Jimmy
Carter the President of Bolivia.

BRINGING BLACK AND WHITE TOGETHER

And then, there was this quote: "If I could find a white man
who had the Negro sound and the Negro feel, I could make
a billion dollars."

So said Sam Phillips, the man who would soon catapult
Presley to glory in the mid-'50s. His words stung all the
more for being true and for saying what they did about a
black man's place in America. Stung so much that two,
three, four decades later, we still felt the pain. What else explains the visceral hostility the black hip-hop community
lavished on a man named Vanilla Ice, a white rap star of
modest talents?

Presley's talents, on the other hand, were prodigious,
which always made it tougher to dismiss him out of hand.
Besides which, there's an inescapable irony in the fact that he
has come to be called an icon of white cultural imperialism
and racial division: In his years of greatest creative power,
Elvis Presley brought black and white together, often at professional risk. Motown, disco and even rap, whose fan base is
as much white as it is black, all grew out of that precedent he
helped to set: the revolutionary idea that black and white
could be brought together in—and by—the groove.

It's worth remembering that Presley arrived during the
last—and in some ways, the fiercest—years of legally man-
dated separation of the races. It was a time when dance or-
ganizers might stretch a rope down the center aisle of an auditorium to keep black and white dancing apart. A time
when police broke up white teen parties because it was
thought the kids were swinging with too much abandon,
swinging too much like Negroes. A time when sweaty white
men with sledgehammers smashed open juke boxes containing music by Negro artists, music variously described as
"animalistic," "jungle-like" and "savage."

What might they have thought to learn that "juke" itself
was an old African word meaning to jab or poke, in a sexual sense? It's probably best they didn't know: The poor
men were already outraged enough, their sense of decency,
their sense of place and self, all under assault by a new

sound emanating from the shanties on the wrong side of the track. Because this was a time of fire.

EXPOSING THE LIE OF SEGREGATION

And Elvis Presley came not to cool that fire, but to stoke it, to make it higher and hotter until it razed the old order and swept away the old men with the sledgehammers where they stood. He married black and white, made country more rhythmic and rhythm more country until what he had sounded like neither and sounded like both. He challenged what had never been challenged before, and the fact that he was a good-looking white boy born among the temples of the old Confederacy only made the act that much more seditious. And subversive. And daring.

Small wonder the establishment reacted to him with such unbridled revulsion. "Unspeakably untalented," said the *New York Herald Tribune.* "Nightmare," said *Look Magazine.* Frank Sinatra called him "deplorable," Jackie Gleason promised that he wouldn't last, Billy Graham said, "I wouldn't let my daughter walk across the street" to see him. And then there's this sign, spotted on a used car lot in Cincinnati: "We guarantee to break 50 Elvis Presley records in your presence if you buy one of these cars today."

It wasn't simply the music that frightened them. It was what the music meant.

Elvis Presley brought separations together, resolved in one grand sweep the irresolution and interdependence of the black and white South. And he revealed segregation as a lie, unmasked white men doing what white men had done since the days of Thomas Jefferson and before: standing at the fence hole spying on black culture, taking notes. Unable to turn away, they stood there conjuring fantasies that blasted and offended their puritanical souls. The thing is, Elvis dared to live what he had conjured. With every throbbing quiver of his leg, every percolating note of rhythm guitar, with every whisper of loss, hymn of grace, thunder of righteousness from his outsized voice, he spoke what was then an officially unspeakable truth: that black and white are intertwined, entangled, woven together like braids.

Which is why James Brown's observation that Elvis "taught white America to get down" comes short of ultimate truth. What Elvis taught didn't stop with getting down, or even with white America.

THE THIRD MOST POPULAR BLACK ARTIST OF THE 1950s

Consider: According to *Billboard Magazine,* Presley was the third most popular black music artist of the 1950s, after Fats Domino and Dinah Washington. Between 1956 and 1963, he posted 24 Top 10 hits on the R&B chart. "Hound Dog," Presley's version of Big Mama Thornton's 1953 hit, spent six weeks at No. 1 in 1956.

And black people, antennae preternaturally attuned to currents of culture and nuances of behavior, sensed something in him the charts could not quantify. Something sweet and genuine, something that respected and admired them. And they responded in kind. Upon spotting Presley one day, black girls on storied Beale Street in Memphis took off after him "like scalded cats," according to a black reporter. The black press noted with approval the way Elvis profusely and publicly thanked a Memphis friend, B.B. King, for "the early lessons."

In his book, "Last Train To Memphis," Peter Guralnik recalls how *Jet* magazine once undertook to verify Presley's rumored disparagement of black people ("The only thing Negroes can do for me is buy my records and shine my shoes."). Presley denied making the statement and *Jet* found no end of black acquaintances willing to vouch for him.

They seem small gestures now. Even Presley's black chart success has been repeated (though less spectacularly) by such white performers as Teena Marie, the Doobie Brothers and Hall and Oates. But in its time, in the days of fire, this was revolution.

And on the anniversary of Presley's death, it seems that the least we can do is remember these things and honor him for them. Elvis Presley has, after all, become rather a foolish figure these last years—a tabloid mainstay kept alive by kitsch, an army of impersonators in rhinestone jumpsuits and the unwillingness of the easily gulled to believe him truly dead.

ELVIS'S MIRACLE

So it seems only fair to remind ourselves that whatever else he was, he was also this: one of the most dangerous men of a very dangerous time, a performer who dared integrate the two pieces of a disparate whole and tell the truth about what it means to be American. He forced raw-boned, hill-country white to look into kinky-haired, son-of-Africa black and see its own reflection. More, he forced us all to see a shared legacy of hardscrabble days and sweltering nights, of loving and longing and guitar twang, of train whistle and mule-drawn plow and front porch lemonade, of pea-picking and Moon Pie and the kind of yearning you can't speak, the kind that starts high in the throat as a keening sound and ends up low in the soul as a weary sigh.

This was music, yes. But it was also miracle.

Twenty years ago Elvis Presley died and I thought it didn't matter.

I was wrong.

CHAPTER 4

Isolation
and Decline

The Army Years

Adam Woog

On December 20, 1957, Elvis received his army induction notice, and he did not return to his musical
career until 1960. Biographer Adam Woog chronicles
the media attention that surrounded Elvis's army induction, his eighteen-month assignment to Bremerhaven, Germany, and his eventual release from the
army in 1960. Woog particularly notes the devastat-
ing effect that Gladys Presley's death had on her son
shortly after he was drafted. Some Elvis biographers
have suggested that Elvis's conscription was the government's response to Elvis's success and his image
as a rebel, and that after his stint in the army Elvis
ceased to be as defiant. Woog, however, notes that
Elvis enjoyed enormous commerical success while
he was in the army. Elvis's core audience remained
loyal, and the singer was welcomed back to stardom
in February 1960.

The fall of 1957 was an unsettling period for Presley. His career was going unbelievably well, but his mother's increasingly poor health—she had been ill for some time and was
drinking heavily—left him depressed. Also, the draft was
hanging over his head.

If he had wanted it, Elvis could have had the armed forces
make him a special case. He could have fulfilled his duty by
entertaining the troops, as many famous performers had
done during the Second World War. The navy wanted to
form a special Elvis company; the air force wanted him to
tour recruiting centers. But the Colonel thought that it was
important for Presley's regular-guy image to accept the same
treatment as everyone else.

In public, Elvis kept his cool about the draft. When the
notice came just before Christmas, he picked it up at the
board offices and then casually dropped by Sun Studios,

cheerfully saying, "Hey, I'm going in." He told reporters that he was ready to serve his country, that he was grateful for the chance to pay back everything that America had given him.

With friends, though, he was franker. He feared that the public wouldn't remember him when he got out and fretted that the Colonel should have arranged a special deal for him. His friends tried to take his mind off it, saying that the government wouldn't let him go—he earned too much and paid too many taxes. (The Colonel often told reporters that it was his "patriotic duty" to keep Elvis in the 90 percent tax bracket.) But the reassurances were of little use. . . .

The draft board granted Presley's request for a delay so he could shoot his next film, *King Creole.* Shortly after his twenty-third birthday, he arrived in California with a large contingent of friends, bodyguards, and business associates.

King Creole was another strong dramatic vehicle, this one about a poor New Orleans waiter who gradually gets involved with mobsters. It was Elvis's favorite of all his movies, and the first to be filmed partly on location in Louisiana. . . .

When shooting was over, Elvis returned to Memphis and crammed as much fun as possible into his remaining time. He saw movies, went roller-skating, organized football games with his pals, went shopping for cars and records. The night before his induction, he and his latest girlfriend, former beauty queen Anita Wood, went with some friends to a drive-in movie and stayed up all night.

Early the next morning, March 24, he arrived at the draft board with his parents and several carloads of friends. A couple of dozen reporters and photographers were already waiting in the light rain. Elvis told them he was very nervous. By 7:15 he was on a bus with twelve other inductees, headed to the Veterans Hospital for examinations and processing. The Colonel stood outside the hospital, handing out balloons advertising *King Creole.*

FORT CHAFFEE

When processing was over, the inductees boarded a bus for Fort Chaffee, Arkansas, 150 miles away. As his mother and father wept, Private Elvis Presley, serial number 53 310 761, called out to his girlfriend, "Goodbye, baby." To the limousine that had brought him, he called out, "Goodbye, you long

Elvis Presley stops to admire the pin of a young fan. During his time in the army, Presley continued to be worshipped by fans of all ages.

black sonofabitch." Elvis was in the army now; he had gone from a monthly income of $100,000 to $78.

Despite Presley's publicly stated wish to be treated like any other soldier, the first days of army life were a circus. His slightest move was painstakingly recorded for a curious public. Some 100 civilians and 50 newsmen, plus 200 dependents of military personnel, were waiting at Fort Chaffee. Dozens of photographers surrounded Elvis at every turn. One even tried to hide in the barracks to get a snapshot of him in bed.

After a few hours of sleep, the new recruits were up at 5:30, only to endure the newsmen—and the Colonel—tagging along for breakfast, five hours of tests and a series of lectures. When a reporter asked what he'd do with the seven dollars in partial pay he received, Elvis smiled and said he would start a loan company. Presley also said his barracks mates were treating him as well as any other new recruit. "They've been swell to me. . . . They consider themselves for what they are— just GIs—the same as me. That's the way I want it."

Then came another ritual for any new soldier: the haircut. Elvis's trim was surely the most-photographed and most-written-about haircut in history. He smiled for the fifty-five newsmen surrounding him and, as his famous locks fell to the floor, muttered, "Hair today, gone tomorrow." A special detail of soldiers swept up the hair and destroyed it to keep it away from fans.

BASIC TRAINING

Presley was assigned to the Second Armored Division at Fort Hood, outside Killeen, Texas. He traveled there by bus, by-passing the usual stops because of the crowds. When his bus stopped at a restaurant in Hillsboro, Texas, two big soldiers were assigned to sit on either side of him; it took twenty-five minutes for someone to recognize him. A small riot ensued, and the waitresses were fighting over his chair as the soldiers fought their way out. Elvis made up for the fuss by buying cigarettes and candy for everyone.

At Fort Hood, newsmen were allowed in for one day, and then Private Presley was strictly off-limits. This allowed him to get on with being a soldier, which he did quite competently; soon he had been awarded a marksman medal and a sharp-shooter medal, and was named acting assistant squad leader.

Given the standard two weeks' leave after two months of training, he went eagerly back to Graceland and his family. He told reporters he was happy to eat his mother's cooking again: "I've eaten things in the Army that I never ate before, and I've eaten things that I didn't know what it was, but after a hard day of basic training, you could eat a rattlesnake."

While in Memphis he wore his uniform because he was proud of it. RCA released the first of Elvis's greatest-hits LPs and his twenty-second single, "Wear My Ring Around Your Neck." And *King Creole* opened to excellent reviews. Even the normally disdainful New York Times liked it: "As the lad himself might say, cut my legs off and call me Shorty! Elvis Presley can act." . . .

THE DEATH OF GLADYS

Colonel Parker had discovered that soldiers could live off base if they had legal dependents, which Vernon and Gladys were.

Elvis was eager to live with his parents in their own house, rather than in the crowded barracks. So he and the elder Presleys, plus Minnie Mae, Vernon's mother, moved to a rented house in Killeen, near the base. Elvis spent his evenings there and often traveled on weekend leaves to see friends in Waco.

But Gladys was increasingly ill. The problem was twofold: a weak heart and hepatitis, a serious liver disease. Both were aggravated by long-term abuse of diet pills and alcohol. On August 8 Vernon took Gladys to Memphis for tests, but she collapsed at home and was admitted to Baptist Memorial Hospital.

When Elvis asked for leave to go see her, his commanding officer at first was reluctant to let him go. He worried that the press would accuse him of granting special privileges. But Gladys's doctor insisted, and late on August 12 Presley arrived at the hospital.

Vernon was sleeping on a cot next to her bed. Elvis spent the night and the whole next day there as well, finally leaving at midnight to get some sleep at home. But then, at 3:30 A.M. on August 14, he was awakened by a phone call. She had taken a turn for the worse. By the time Elvis got there, his mother was dead.

On their knees beside the bed, weeping openly, Elvis and his father waited until the hearse arrived to take her away and then went home. By the time reporters found them at Graceland, they were sitting on the steps with their arms around each other. "She's all we lived for," Elvis told them. "She was always my best girl."

Hundreds of well-wishers had gathered at the Graceland gates by the time her body was brought to the house. Telegrams and letters of condolence—over one hundred thousand in all—began arriving. Gladys's body was moved the next day to a funeral home, where thousands came to pay their respects.

Elvis was inconsolable for weeks. His leave was extended, but finally he had to return to Fort Hood. Before he left, he left instructions that nothing in his mother's room was to be changed. He even ordered that the pane of glass she had fallen against when she collapsed was not to be repaired.

Gradually, Presley had to pull himself together and get on with his life. He had received word that in September he and fourteen hundred other soldiers were sailing for duty in West Germany. The 1950s were a time of great tension between the

Western powers and Communist East Germany, and there was constant fear that East Germany might launch an invasion to the west. The American military was a forceful presence in West Germany, and Presley's tank unit would be part of it.

To Germany

Late that year, Private Presley traveled by train to New York to board his ship for Germany. The scene awaiting him at

---

Did the Colonel Want Elvis to Be Drafted?

In his biography of Elvis, Albert Goldman contends that Elvis was only drafted because, on the advice of his manager Colonel Tom Parker, he volunteered to take the army's preinduction physical exam in January 1957. As a result he was classified as fit for service and drafted within the year. Goldman believes that Parker hoped military service would improve Elvis's image and curtail his growing independence.

As to the question of why the Colonel should have urged Elvis to interrupt his career at its peak in order to join an army that was in no hurry to draft him, we find ourselves up against one of the most baffling questions posed by Colonel Parker's mysterious machinations. We do know that during this period, Elvis had come to take a very condescending and even antagonistic view of the Colonel and his activities. Elvis told one of his close friends in Texas, Eddie Fadal, that "anybody could do my booking because it ain't that much of a job, scheduling me." Elvis could have said as much to other people and the word gotten back to the Colonel, who kept Elvis surrounded always with a network of spies. It is possible that the Colonel, who had found Elvis such a simple and easy-to-manage lad, was now becoming fearful that the boy was taking off in the same direction as the character he portrayed in *Jailhouse Rock*. Could the con who runs the rackets in the big house and who the kid reduces eventually to his flunky be a disguised portrait of the Colonel and a prophecy of his future role in the Presley camp? . . . Perhaps the whole army nightmare, of which the Colonel did make extensive use to change Elvis's image, was at bottom a device to cut the King of Rock 'n' Roll down to size. If that was its purpose, it succeeded brilliantly. As John Lennon remarked when he was informed that Elvis had died—"Elvis died the day he went into the army."

Albert Goldman, *Elvis*, 1981.

the Brooklyn Army Terminal was riotous. Over a hundred newsmen, a squad of RCA executives, Vernon, Anita, the Colonel, and dozens of others were assembled for a giant, hour-long press conference.

He finally was able to march up the ship's gangplank, waving and carrying a duffle bag. The band played "Tutti Frutti," thousands on shore screamed, and cameras snapped. He had to walk up the gangplank eight times before the newsmen were satisfied. On board, he recorded a Christmas message for his fans, which, together with an edited version of the press conference, the Colonel issued on record as "Elvis Sails!"

On deck, Elvis handed out souvenir postcards and pictures and threw kisses to shore. When he playfully buckled his knees and snapped his fingers, the crowd erupted. And then he was gone. As the *New York Herald-Tribune* put it, "His admirers shrieked. Colonel Parker beamed. The Department of Defense man from Washington who had overseen the operation wiped his brow and sighed."

Elvis records were already big sellers in Germany, and a crowd of five hundred was waiting for him when his ship landed in Bremerhaven on October 1. But Presley was hustled onto a train and taken to his post outside Friedberg, a small town in central Germany. The base officers held a three-day "open house" for crowds of reporters, then declared their famous charge off-limits.

He was assigned to be a scout jeep driver. Scouts were needed to travel the countryside by jeep and provide information on road conditions, so that if an invasion did occur, Western tanks would not find themselves trapped by unusable roads.

Private Presley was a model soldier. Since he was still allowed to live off base with his dependents, his father and grandmother joined him in a modest, middle-class home near the base. Usually, he was awake at 5:00 or 5:30 in the morning and not home again until 5:00 P.M. or later. A sign outside his house read: "Autographs between 7:30 and 8:30 P.M."

The army didn't affect Elvis's earnings or popularity as badly as he had feared. Elvis earned two million dollars for the year 1958, though he had been a soldier almost the entire time. He got ten thousand letters a week, some of them marked simply "Elvis, U.S. Army." Still, RCA was worried about the scarcity of new material, and what remained had been carefully doled out. By February 1959, the unreleased material was getting thin: there were no Presley songs on *Billboard*'s "Hot 100" for the first time in almost three years.

In March 1959, the company issued "A Fool Such as I," his nineteenth consecutive million-seller. The last of the unreleased material, "A Big Hunk o' Love," came out in June— the same month Presley was promoted to specialist fourth class. To make up for the lack of new material, RCA repackaged old songs and found that they sold nearly as well.

In August Colonel Parker announced that Presley's first post-army film would be about—surprise!—an army tank sergeant stationed in Germany. It was to be called *G.I. Blues,* and it would again team Elvis with producer Hal Wallis.

The money was rolling in, but not fast enough; everyone was eager for Elvis to get out. Near the end of the wait, the Colonel had a fake newspaper printed up. A huge banner headline read ELVIS RE-ENLISTS; underneath it was a smaller headline, WALLIS COLLAPSES. The Colonel wrapped it around Wallis's paper in Los Angeles and left it on the producer's front steps one morning. Wallis read the main headline and really did collapse before he got around to looking at the smaller headline.

OUT AT LAST

Life in the army was mostly routine, but not everything was dreary. Elvis became interested in karate and worked his way up to a second-degree black belt. He also met a very special girl: Priscilla Beaulieu, the fourteen-year-old daughter of an air force officer. They began dating regularly. In time, Elvis would become as obsessed with Priscilla as he had once been with his mother.

In early 1960 Presley was promoted to sergeant and began commanding a three-man reconnaissance team. Then came news that he would be discharged in February, a month early. The media immediately snapped into action: there were magazine contests, special radio programs, and a rerelease of *Jailhouse Rock.* Plans were made to press a million copies of his first post-army single before it was even recorded. And it was announced that Elvis's first public appearance on a Frank Sinatra television special would earn him $125,000—more than any other TV guest had ever received.

The day before he left Germany, he took part in another huge press conference. The big surprise there was the presence of Marion Keisker, his old friend from Sun Records and one of the people most responsible for bringing Elvis to public attention.

Keisker was now a captain in the air force, assigned to the Armed Forces Television network in Germany. When they met, Keisker said, "Hi, hon." Elvis was astonished: he cried, "Marion! In Germany! And an officer! What do I do? Kiss you or salute you?" She replied, "In that order." The officer in charge of the proceedings was disturbed by this lack of respect for a superior officer; Elvis explained that if Keisker had not thought to make an extra tape recording one day in Memphis, none of them would have been there.

Priscilla saw Elvis off at the Frankfurt airport. He landed at Fort Dix, New Jersey, to find a snowstorm and, of course, a gang of newsmen. After yet another huge press conference (during which Elvis's casual remark that he probably would grow his sideburns back sent reporters sprinting for the phones), Presley was formally discharged.

He had done his service to his country and was once again a civilian. Now it remained to be seen whether he could resume his sidetracked career.

Elvis in Hollywood

Bill Reed

Music critic Bill Reed traces Elvis's career as an actor from his first film in 1956 through to the late
1960s. Elvis initially enjoyed working on films, Reed
notes, and seems to have had aspirations of becoming a serious actor. However, most Elvis movies after
his thirteenth film, *Kissin' Cousins,* were low-budget,
inanely plotted musicals designed to turn a quick
profit and sell more albums. Reed writes that Elvis
had an ambiguous relationship with Hollywood: He
loved the movies, but disliked life in Hollywood; his
films were almost uniformly bad, but they were also
enormously profitable.

"I feel like a bird who's been let out of his cage and wants to
fly a little. I want to flap my wings. I want to feel sure I'm free
again. I never know what I want to do, but I sure want to do
something that has nothing to do with this (movie) business."

—Elvis Presley

When Elvis Presley went to Hollywood in 1956 to make *Love
Me Tender,* he and his aides checked in at the Beverly
Wilshire Hotel for an unusually lengthy stay. For earlier
West Coast recording sessions with RCA, Elvis had touched
down briefly at places like the Knickerbocker and Roosevelt
hotels, where his visits always triggered pandemonium. At
the Beverly Wilshire it was more apparent than ever that hotel living in Hollywood would never cut it on a long-term basis. Still, from April of '56 until the autumn of the following
year Elvis and his down home crew mostly camped out
there—even though the scene in the hotel's lobby consti-
tuted a *fan*atical obstacle course.

The novelty of whooping it up (with room service yet!)
still hadn't worn off. Elvis, Alan Fortas, Red West, and others
of Elvis' aides and cronies were still humorously getting off
on the attention and pranks of the almost exclusively female

horde of lurking, pouncing Presley fans who had to be literally—as they say—beaten off with a stick.

Even if Elvis *could* have engaged in normal rounds of partygoing and nightlife he probably wouldn't have. For the innate country boy in him caused him to feel generally uncomfortable around most of the Hollywood "types" he met during the day while making movies. In fact, almost immediately after his first lengthy exposure to the movie capital, he put it down publicly. At a press conference back home in Memphis during a break in the filming of *Love Me Tender* he spoke very bitterly of Hollywood, stating that he'd never want to live there permanently. In so many words he expressed the opinion that he wasn't *ever* going to let the bright-lights-big-city atmosphere of tinsel town cause him to forget that when all was said and done his heart belonged to Memphis, Tennessee. A little more than a year later, though, Elvis' heart would belong to Uncle Sam. He entered the Army in March, 1958, and for the next two years the theoretical and practical problems of "going Hollywood" were temporarily defused.

When Elvis was mustered out of the service in 1960 he immediately went back to making movies. His first post-Army film, naturally enough, was *G.I. Blues,* and perhaps the only person who *wasn't* surprised at how successful it was (even more so than *Love Me Tender*) was Colonel Tom Parker. If ever there was any doubt that Elvis Presley was a long-range movie phenomenon, *G.I. Blues* effectively dispelled it. For the foreseeable future, Elvis would be spending as much time, if not more so, in the movie capital as back home at Graceland. Hotel living this time around was obviously out of the question.

The year of *G.I. Blues,* 1960, Elvis and his entourage (not yet known as the "Memphis Mafia," but beginning to be called El's Angels) moved into the first of four rented homes they would occupy throughout most of the 1960's. All were located either in or near Beverly Hills or Bel Air. (When Elvis married he finally bought a house in Los Angeles' exclusive Truesdale Estates section.) The first house was at 565 Perugia Way, adjacent to the Bel Air Country Club golf course. One of Elvis' neighbors was another early rock and roller (of sorts)—Pat Boone. Also living nearby was "Mrs. Minniver," Greer Garson. The house was a pseudo-oriental affair, built in a semi-circle around a garden and a waterfall.

The first thing Elvis did when he moved in was to rip out the garden, replace it with a "rec" room, which he then proceeded to fill up with pool tables, a jukebox and other leisure time accoutrements. (Since Elvis couldn't go out for fun and games it's little wonder he made adequate provisions for "r and r" right off the bat.)

By the time Elvis moved into the Perugia Way compound, the potential for precipitating a riot should he go out in public was even greater than during the earlier years. Not only were restaurants and nightclubs totally out of bounds, but so too was movie going, one of Elvis' favorite pastimes.

"I'M A MOVIE FAN"

In an early fan magazine interview, Elvis said, "I go to the movies. I'm a movie fan. Me and the boys take off at any time to take in a movie, there isn't a weekend we don't take in two. We go to any movie house. I've seen some movies a half-a-dozen times when it's got something to say by way of interesting acting."

By 1960, though, the possibility of visiting just "any movie house" was an utter impossibility. But like the mountain and Mohammed, if Elvis couldn't go to the movies, the movies would have to come to Elvis.

Private home screenings in Hollywood are nothing unusual. Most of that town's successful industry officials and celebrities enjoyed home movie viewing. But Elvis, of course, really outdid himself. Just as in Memphis where he rented the Memphian Theatre for all-night movie parties on a fairly regular basis, similarly in Hollywood most of Elvis' nights at home with friends and employees included the showing of at least one movie. (This at a time before home video when showing films was a moderately complex and cumbersome affair.)

Some of the films cropping up most frequently at these movie parties were Elvis' personal favorites. These included: *To Kill a Mockingbird, Lawrence of Arabia, Diamonds Are Forever, Straw Dogs, Rebel Without a Cause, The Godfather*—and later a special favorite for which Elvis shared his enthusiasm with Richard Nixon, *Patton*. Most of these titles are on the downbeat/fantastical/violent side, but they constitute a fairly erudite selection. Surprisingly though, the film Elvis showed most frequently was Blake Edwards' amiable knockabout comedy, *The Party*. The reason being that, wonder of wonders,

Elvis' favorite movie performer wasn't Clint Eastwood, James Dean or Spencer Tracy (all of whom he appreciated unceasingly) BUT, *The Party*'s star, Peter Sellers. (It seems like an unlikely choice even after you think about it for a while.) Elvis was also fond of Edwards and Sellers' *A Shot in the Dark.*

To underscore just how much of a film fan Elvis was, many times during his Las Vegas shows he would often veer off into lengthy and uncannily accurate renderings of scenes from favorite films. One that cropped up often was Marlon Brando's "Don Corleone" death scene from *The Godfather.*

A GOSSIP COLUMNIST'S DREAM

Sometimes upwards of a hundred people were invited to Elvis' "at-homes," which generally were highlighted by the showing of a film or two. The evening didn't officially begin until the host had made his entrance, with guests tending to hold themselves in a kind of pre-party holding pattern until then. Finally, at least at the Perugia Way house, the walls would literally part—Red Sea fashion—to reveal Elvis elaborately costumed. After surveying the room momentarily, Elvis would slowly enter into the goings-on. It was a show biz "entrance" in every sense of the word.

Invariably the males in the room were outnumbered by the females, many of whom were part of a whole elaborate pecking order of sexual liaisons to be gone through before (at some later date) finally getting to bed down with Presley himself. In the early Hollywood years, the parties never approached being wild or orgiastic—in keeping with Elvis' proprietous self-image. Generally on hand too for these often large but always casual affairs was Elvis' current girlfriend, who as likely as not turned out to be his on-screen love interest of the film he was working on at the time.

During the years prior to Elvis' marriage to Priscilla in 1967 Elvis was publicly reported as being romantically involved with a lengthy list of stars and starlets—this was near the end of the era of that happy breed. Gossip columnists' tongues wagged over Elvis pitching woo with such of his co-stars as: Tuesday Weld *(Wild in the Country);* Ursula Andress *(Fun in Acapulco);* Yvonne Craig *(Kissin' Cousins, It Happened at the World's Fair)* and Ann-Margret *(Viva Las Vegas).* There was also Nancy Sinatra from *Speedway.* The mind reels over what Papa Frank might've thought about Elvis as a prospective son-in-law. (Ironically Nancy Sinatra ended up wedding early Elvis clone, singer Tommy Sands.)

Elvis also dated Natalie Wood (one of the few of his girl-friends honored with an invite to Graceland), Roger Corman starlet Yvonne Lime and Raquel Welch, whose first movie part was a walk-on in Elvis' *Roustabout.*

And there was the one that got away, Debra Paget, Elvis' *amour* in *Love Me Tender.* Small wonder she tried to (and successfully) elude her co-star's advances. For she just happened to be dating an even more powerful king from another domain at the time—Howard Hughes. (The potential combo of Presley and Hughes surely constituting two-thirds of the equivalent of a grand slam in the game of romantic triangles.)

KISSIN' COUSINS

Throughout the early sixties the parties continued, and up until the time of *Kissin' Cousins* (1964), Elvis was reported to still have been enthused by film work. He was quite proud of his straight acting role in Don Siegel's *Flaming Star* (1960), and he was also pleased by the job he'd done in *King Creole* (originally intended for James Dean), the last film he completed before entering the service. *Wild in the Country* (1961) also finds an Elvis still trying to hone his acting skills. However, even then, three full years before the disastrous *Kissin' Cousins,* there were apparently already some doubts as to whether Elvis would be allowed to carry on as a "serious" actor.

Phillip Dunne, the director of *Wild in the Country,* recalls in his autobiography, *Take Two,* the various ways in which front office intervention helped botch this project, with its script by prominent playwright Clifford Odets. 20th-Century-Fox, for example, insisted that songs be inserted into the plot, no matter how unnecessary they were for plot development. Part way through the film's shooting a rushed schedule was instituted, at which time the film's budget was also suddenly slashed. All of this wreaked havoc on a film that Dunne (and Presley) hoped would help establish Presley once and for all as a respectable straight actor. (Even with all the tampering Elvis' acting skills still manage to come across in the film.)

Most of Elvis' films during the next three years following *Wild in the Country,* including *Kid Galahad, Girls! Girls!*

Although Elvis enjoyed working on his early films, such as Jailhouse Rock, *he eventually grew tired of formulaic roles.*

Girls! and *Follow That Dream*, were nothing to write home about. For sheer tattiness, though, none of them could compare with the crucial *Kissin' Cousins* (1964), produced by that cut-rate movie expert, Sam *(Rock Around the Clock)* Katzman.

Colonel Parker linked up with Katzman after he'd observed the impressive grosses for the producer's film of the life story of Hank Williams. (Elvis had once considered playing the lead in this film, *Your Cheatin' Heart*, which ended up being one of the better grossing films of 1964.) Watching the success of Katzman's country music bio, Parker for the first time became intrigued with the potential bottom line profits if he placed Elvis before the cameras in the same kind of quickie venture as was Katzman's stock-in-trade. And so he hired on the "B" movie producer to oversee Presley's next picture.

Every movie of Elvis' prior to *Kissin' Cousins* had been a quality affair, typified by relatively lengthy shooting schedules and fairly generous budgets. Suddenly, with this new approach, Elvis' films began costing one-third to one-fourth of what they had before. *Kissin' Cousins,* for example, had a shooting schedule of only seventeen days—about the amount of time it takes to make a run-of-the-mill made-for-TV movie.

It didn't take long for Elvis to realize what was happening; and after their friend's death many of those closest to Elvis have noted that his single greatest disappointment in life was that he didn't get a chance to prove himself as an actor.

Apparently, though, Elvis didn't entirely give in to the Colonel without a struggle, for all the while he was appearing in the post–*Kissin' Cousins* embarrassments he was taking at least tentative steps to get himself back on the right track. To exactly what extent Elvis went with these efforts are facets of The Elvis Presley Story already lost to the dim recesses of Hollywood lore. In later years Elvis is said to have been seriously interested in being a part of at least two more "respectable" film projects, *Midnight Cowboy* and *A Star Is Born.* (In the years before the three-pictures-a-year routine set in Elvis was sought out for and/or wanted roles in such prestige projects as *How the West Was Won* and *West Side Story.* His first movie *was* to have been the "classy" *The Rainmaker,* with Katharine Hepburn and Burt Lancaster; and almost immediately upon arriving in Hollywood for *Love Me Tender* there was talk of a film bio of the life of James Dean, to star Elvis.)

With the exception of Elvis' last two films, which were concert movies, seldom did films number 14–31 ever deviate from the formula hit on with *Kissin' Cousins,* i.e. exotic locale, curvaceous cuties literally draped over the sets, an inane action-filled script and a neat LP's worth of songs. (Elvis' excellent 15th film, *Viva Las Vegas,* though released after *Kissin' Cousins,* was actually shot prior to it.)

THE JERRYBUILT, ASSEMBLY LINE NATURE OF ELVIS' LATER FILMS

It is almost a cliche today to speak of how bad Elvis' later films were, but even *while* they were being turned out strong reaction had set in against them. Newspaper reviews when they appeared at all were nearly uniformly damning; and even *Elvis Monthly* had stopped running articles about their idol's films, stating that they were "puppet shows for not overbright children."

No one is entirely certain how much money these "puppet shows" brought in, but some estimates place the *profits* at over $200,000,000. (Elvis also co-owned the music publishing rights of his films.) Only when audience interest in these affairs dropped off with *Charro* and *Change of Habit* was the decision made to stop grinding them out.

In the Elvis memorial issue of *Rolling Stone* magazine, Don Siegel, the director of *Flaming Star* (which some consider Elvis' best film) related the obstacle course he had to run in order to get a quality film made. Recalled Siegel, "I found him very sensitive and very good, with the exception that he was very unsure of himself. Very insecure. He felt he could have done better things. And his advisors—namely the Colonel—were very much against doing this kind of (straight) role. They tried to get him to sing throughout the picture. (Note: The film ended up with only a title tune over the credits.) Obviously they didn't want him to get off a winning horse. But when I was able to calm him down, I thought he gave a beautiful performance."

In the same issue of *Rolling Stone*, Norman Taurog, the director of *nine* Presley features, echoed Siegel's sentiments by saying that he felt Elvis "never reached his peak." Taurog passed away in 1979, and with his death went a treasure trove of Elvis' oral history. To term Taurog a "director," though, is a bit of a misnomer, for by the time he came on the scene the part he played in the making of the films was more akin to that of a traffic cop and/or camp counselor. Yes, to allay the boredom of the daily moviemaking grind (and of the films themselves) Elvis and his retinue regularly engaged in katzenjammer hi-jinks such as cherry bomb throwing, karate antics, water bombs, shaving cream battles and chasing one another around the set with Bic lighters which had the tips cut off them, altering them into miniature flame throwers. (To underscore his impatience with the shabby film projects Elvis once sardonically remarked, "Hey, there are some pretty funny things in this script. I'm going to have to read it some day.")

Although Elvis worked on heavily guarded closed sets, sometimes important visitors were allowed to watch the filming of his pictures. "El's Angels" were probably on their best behavior when such visiting *non*–show business royalty as the kings and queens of Nepal and Thailand and princesses from Denmark, Norway and Sweden dropped by.

The recollections of writer George Kirgo, the author (with Theodore Flicker) of *Spinout* (1966)—one of the better of the quickies—points up the jerrybuilt, assembly line aspect of Elvis' later films. The writing team had originally been assigned to concoct a feature for Sonny and Cher. Just as Kirgo and Flicker got to work writing the film, they received a call from MGM, their producers, requesting that they write something for Elvis instead. Kirgo still doesn't know why the Bonos' movie was cancelled, but he recalls, "We finished the script and turned it in and a few days later we were called into a meeting with Colonel Parker. He *loved* the script—except for one thing. 'Put a dog in it,' he said. And so we went back and put a dog in it. Then a few days later we got a call from MGM back on the East Coast telling us to put a race car in it." (Initially, you see, *Spinout* wasn't a racing picture at all.)

Kirgo also remembers the film's first three distinctly non-auto working titles. At first it was called *Always At Midnight*. Then it was known as *Never Say Yes*, which was *then* slightly

---

ELVIS AND THE JUVENILIZATION OF AMERICAN MOVIES
Music historian James Miller suggests that the success of Elvis's movies helped make Hollywood filmmakers realize that one way to make films more profitable was to gear them to relatively unsophisticated teen audiences.

Elvis Presley figured in three of the top twenty films of 1957: *Love Me Tender* (number ten, originally released in November 1956, grossing a cumulative $4.5 million at the box office), *Loving You* (number nineteen, released in July 1957, grossing $3.7 million), and *Jailhouse Rock* (number fifteen, grossing $3.7 million by the end of the year). Low-budget films like *Rock, Pretty Baby; Don't Knock the Rock;* and *Rock, Rock, Rock!* also returned handsome profits.

By 1958, the long-term implications of these facts were just beginning to dawn on filmmakers. The taste of kids was going to play a large role in calling the shots in Hollywood, as it already did in Tin Pan Alley. A front page headline in *Variety* put it this way: "Film Future: GI Baby Boom." One of the experts that *Variety* quoted, Arno H. Johnson, vice president and senior economist for the J. Walter Thompson Company, predicted

adjusted to *Never Say No*. None of these titles were Kirgo and Flicker's; but the final one of *Spinout* was Kirgo's. "It was left over," he explains, "from an earlier race car picture I'd written for Howard Hawks, who nixed it at the last minute in favor of *Red Line 7,000*."

Kirgo never actually met Elvis until the final day of the film's shooting. "The producers asked Ted Flicker and myself if we'd like to meet Elvis. Naturally we said yes, and we went on to the set. It was a very brief meeting. He was very polite, and thanked us for the script. He said it was very good. Then he reached over to a stack of the most hideous . . . most horrible fake oil paintings of himself I've ever seen. Ghastly! Then he signed one and handed it to me." And that was the extent of meetings between the star and his screenwriters. All of five minutes; and at the *end* of the shooting.

LIFE IN HOLLYWOOD

By the time of *Spinout* in 1966 Elvis and his retainers had been leading an increasingly nomadic existence in the film community. In 1963, it was decided that the Perugia Way house just wasn't large enough so Elvis and his crew pulled

---

that "the growth of the 'teen market' is bound to make itself felt in many areas, but nowhere is it of greater significance than in the film field, both in terms of audience potential and as a guide to motion picture content. Not only are these the future homemakers, but they represent the 'restless' element of the population, the people who don't want to stay home and watch TV and who are still immune to any sophisticated disdain of run-of-the-mill screen offerings."

In other words, kids wouldn't care about a crappy film, they wouldn't know any better (being immune to "sophisticated disdain"—a great way to describe the discerning exercise of judgment).

But Mr. Johnson was right. And thanks to the mind-boggling mediocrity of almost all of his highly profitable films, Elvis Presley not only squandered the best years of his creative life on drivel and kitsch—he also can take credit for accelerating what one historian has aptly called "the juvenilization of American movies," from *Blackboard Jungle* to *Star Wars*, and beyond.

James Miller, *Flowers in the Dustbin: The Rise of Rock and Roll, 1947–1977*. New York: Simon and Schuster, 1999.

up stakes and moved to a nearby baronial white elephant of a Hollywood-style mansion located at 1059 Bellagio Road in Bel Air. It came complete with a tennis-court-sized marble entrance hall and a bowling alley in the basement. The problem was it was *too* big and just plain creepy—almost immediately the outfit moved back into the old Perugia Way house, where they remained until 1965. After that it was onward to a low-slung modern house at 10050 Rocca Place situated in a cul-de-sac in Stone Canyon near the Bel Air Hotel. This was the house where Elvis and Priscilla would spend the first few months of their married life together before Elvis made the decision to plunk down the money and *buy* his first West Coast house.

The home he bought at 1174 Hillcrest Road was an elaborate multi-level pseudo-French regency affair, with four huge bedrooms, six bathrooms and the requisite Olympic-size swimming pool. This new acquisition was only six years old, and so the $400,000 purchase price was considered a "steal"—especially since it was located in the exclusive Truesdale Estates section. High on an uppermost hill, the house was surrounded by cypress trees and commanded a sweeping view of the Los Angeles area. Here in keeping with his new image as a married man, Elvis cut back his "staff" considerably with only Richard Davis and Joe Esposito (from the inner circle) staying on at the Hillcrest address.

Elvis' Hollywood lifestyle had remained more or less the same at all of his "western Gracelands"—only the personnel changed from time to time, with the one constant being Elvis' semi-legendary and highly destructive alcoholic chimpanzee, Scatter. (Elvis bought him after seeing him on a TV show.) The TV was on constantly, the movie screenings and dates with co-stars continued, and Sunday touch football games became an institution at De Neve Park in Bel Air.

This weekend pastime of Elvis and his pals came on like an early version of TV celebrity sports shows. With a rag tag football crew consisting of, among others, Ty Hardin, Ricky Nelson, Kent McCord, Gary Lockwood, Dean Torrance (of Jan and Dean), Max Baer, Jr. and Robert Conrad (reportedly Pat Boone even showed up on occasion but his wife Shirley would anxiously come to fetch him before the game was over), the football games offered up not just Elvis for all the world to see, but an impressive array of TV's leading men and rock and roll stars. Small wonder then that after a few years the citizens of Bel Air politely requested that Elvis kindly take his game elsewhere, for the ensuing traffic jams and general chaos that usually occurred proved too much for the sedate community.

Favorite activities included filling up the swimming pool with flash bulbs and shooting at them (a sure sign of boredom if there ever was one) and the famed aimless late night rides through the hills of Bel Air and up and down the Sunset Strip with no goal at hand—with Elvis often leading the pack in his Cadillac with its forty coats of diamond and fish scale paint, 24k. gold trim, gold lame drapes, refrigerator, hi-fi, TV and gold-record-bedecked ceiling.

But when he could flee the film capital, Elvis would always kick back at Graceland. The move to Memphis usually consisted of a caravan led by Elvis in his customized mobile home, followed by a flotilla of the faithful in the various swank autos he'd purchased for them. And when his movie career bottomed out and his stage activities took an upswing in the late sixties, most of Elvis' time on the West Coast was spent in Palm Springs, rather than Hollywood—which suited him just fine.

Comeback in Las Vegas

Jerry Hopkins

By the late 1960s, Elvis had tired of starring in light-hearted Hollywood musicals. He wanted to return to singing before a live audience, in the manner that had made him famous. On July 31, 1969, Elvis opened at the International Hotel in Las Vegas—his first live performance since March 1961. The series of sold-out "comeback" Las Vegas performances that followed marked one of the high points in Elvis's career. In the following excerpt from his book *Elvis: A Biography* (written in 1971, when Elvis was still alive), Jerry Hopkins recounts the opening night of Elvis's triumphant return to the stage. Hopkins was one of the first authors to chronicle the life of Elvis.

"I got tired of singing to the guys I beat up in the motion pictures," Elvis said the night he opened in Las Vegas.

So, months earlier, the Colonel had gone to work, negotiating a contract with the International Hotel, a thirty-story building that was to be the largest hotel (1519 rooms) in Las Vegas but then was still under construction. It was, on completion, the first major Las Vegas hotel built off the Strip. It cost $60 million, and at 346 feet was the tallest building in Nevada. It had the world's largest casino, and in the middle of its eight-and-a-half-acre rooftop recreation area was a swimming pool that held 350,000 gallons of water, the largest man-made body of water in the state, aside from Lake Mead. It had 240 miles of carpeting, more than 2500 employees (who were to be paid $25 million the first year), an eighteen-hole golf course, a convention hall that seated 5000, six major dining areas (not counting the Showroom Internationale, which seated 2000 and was to be Elvis's showcase for a month), a thousand slot machines and a computer-operated reservation desk.

It seemed a suitable place for Elvis to use for his public return. . . .

The Showroom Internationale was a masterpiece in ostentation, a monstrous multileveled restaurant and balcony that seated two thousand nearly comfortably and offered as part of the décor a phony Roman colonnade, some larger-than-life-size figures in Louis XIV velvet and lace, paintings of Greek ruins which made a travesty of artistic perspective, and hanging precariously above all this, some scattered cupidlike angels. The menu offered a narrow but gout-inducing selection of wines and foods that began with Fonds d'Artichauts Farcis Walewska and closed with Savarin Glacé Napoléon.

Finally a disembodied voice: "Ladies and gentlemen, welcome to the International Hotel and the Elvis Presley show with Sammy Shore, the Sweet Inspirations and the Imperials."

The gold lamé curtain rose, tucking itself away in the ceiling, to reveal the Bobby Morris orchestra in tuxedos, the four Sweet Inspirations bopping toward the audience, looking much like a road show version of the Supremes, singing show tunes. Sammy Shore came next. He knew the invitation-only crowd was there to see Elvis and he aimed some of his material that way: "The Colonel came up to me and said, 'I like your kind of humor.' I said, 'Why, thank you. I like your chicken.' And the Colonel said, 'You do? Well, lick my fingers.'" And then he said, "Youth is wasted on the young. Give us what the kids got and you know what you'd have? A lot of old people with pimples."

As Sammy was keeping the older folks laughing—boring or antagonizing the younger ones—Elvis stood in the wings. He was drumming his fingers against his thighs nervously. He watched Sammy, probably not seeing or hearing him, then disappeared farther backstage to talk to one of the boys positioned there for security, then he reappeared again, still drumming his fingers.

Sammy closed with a routine that used evangelism as its base, blue humor and a lot of tambourine-banging as its means of delivery, and got off. The curtain fell, there was a frantic moment rolling out the piano and drum kit and getting set, musicians and singers scuttling back and forth, stagehands moving microphones, and then the curtain went up again.

THE ENTRANCE

The band was pounding out a rolling, thunderous "Baby, I Don't Care" rhythm and without a word from the disembodied voice, Elvis sauntered to center stage, grabbed the microphone from its stand, hit a pose from the fifties—legs braced, knees snapping almost imperceptibly—and before he could begin the show that he had pushed through three full-dress rehearsals that afternoon, the audience stopped him cold. Just as he was to begin his first song, he was hit in the face with a roar. He looked. All two thousand people were on their feet, pounding their hands together and whistling, many of them standing on their chairs and screaming. And he hadn't even opened his mouth.

Finally the ovation subsided, the band picked up the beat and Elvis hit the pose again: "Waaaaaaaal, it's one for the money. . . ."

The leg snapped.

"Two for the show . . ."

The leg snapped again, and he thumped his acoustic guitar.

"Three to get ready, now go cat go. . . ."

It was as if the audience had fallen through a time warp, leaving the sixties for the fifties, appearing somewhere on the biting edge of memory that went with high school and the beginnings of rock 'n' roll. It was a shortened version of "Blue Suede Shoes," lasting only a minute and a half, and as the audience was applauding, Elvis walked to his right, toward Charlie Hodge, who handed him a glass of water.

"During the show you'll see I drink a lot of wa-wa," he said, using his daughter's word for water. "That's because the desert air is very dry and it affects my throat. I've also got some Gatorade. It's supposed to act twelve times faster than water." He held the bottle aloft. "Looks as if it's been used already to me . . . but if it aids my gator. . . ."

The comment was made offhandedly in the familiar slurring drawl that had come out of Mississippi and gone through so many movies, emerging nearly fifteen years later as the voice of a relaxed yet polished performer. Backstage the boys were laughing at the joke. "Gatorade . . . used already . . . whew!" Haw haw haw.

Elvis went into his second song, "I Got a Woman," and then, almost as an afterthought, something he'd forgotten, he said, "Good evening, ladies and gentlemen. Welcome to the big, freaky International Hotel, with those weirdo dolls on the walls, and those funky angels on the ceiling . . . and, man, you ain't seen nothin' until you've seen a funky angel."

The next song was "Love Me Tender" and this was for the fans. Elvis spotted a pretty girl near the edge of the stage and knelt down and kissed her. He kissed a second, and a third, and a fourth, working his way along the stage. Still singing.

And from that right into a medley of his early hits—"Jailhouse Rock," "Don't Be Cruel," "Heartbreak Hotel" and "All Shook Up." Here and there the lyrics were altered slightly, as if Elvis was playing with the songs, not regarding them so seriously as perhaps he did in the 1950s.

A Shade of Parody

Then, mock serious, he said, "This is the only song I could think of that really expresses my feelings toward the audience."

He sang "Hound Dog."

It was just the way it had been in the fifties, when "Hound Dog" was the song he used to *close* his shows. The same gutty power was there, along with just a shade of parody. Elvis was singing the song because he enjoyed it and because he thought it funny. Later in the month he would tell the audience, as he went to get some water, "When I drink wa-wa, just say to each other, 'Is that him, is that him? I thought he was bigger than that.'" Elvis knew there was something that was bigger than reality involved: the image. And Elvis was ready to laugh at it.

The next song was "Memories."

After which he looked at the floor and spotted the letters "B.S." in marker pen. "It says 'B.S.' here," he told his audience. "Do you think they're trying to tell me something?" There was scattered laughter. "Oh . . . maybe it stands for Barbra Streisand." There was a roar of laughter.

Right into "My Babe," an up-tempo song that had been a hit for the Righteous Brothers.

Then "I Can't Stop Loving You."

The audience was reacting—creating and distributing energy in massive waves—and Elvis was reacting to that. His voice was deeper, richer, more sensual than it was in ten years of soggy films, guttier even than nostalgia gave it credit for being before the soggy films began. And behind and all around it was the tight, basic yet soulful rhythm of James Burton and his good ol' boys, and the scaling, precisely timed harmony of the Imperials and the Sweet Inspirations, filling in every musical crack, building a melodic yet roughhouse wall of sound.

"I'd like to do my latest release," he said, catching his breath and drinking some Gatorade. "It's been a big seller for me." And then he added modestly, "Something I really needed."

"In the Ghetto."

And from that right into the song he said would be his next single, "Suspicious Minds." Elvis was forty minutes into his show and the audience was in disarray. Bouffants were tilting, neckties askew. People were sweating. Women were wriggling on the edge of their seats, debating whether or not to make a dash for it. Elvis was wearing a modified karate suit, tied at the waist and slashed down the front, all black. With all that black, black hair covering the tops of his ears, shaggy, almost Beatle-length, the lean features of his face, and the moves—the legs spreading, stretching, actually *vibrating*—it was enough to make any female itch. All that was needed was a final push.

A six-minute version of "Suspicious Minds" provided it. In this, a heavy production number utilizing the full orchestra, Elvis told the story of getting "caught in a trap," loving a girl and knowing it couldn't go on—with suspicious minds. He also turned the stage into a karate mat, kicking and slashing and tumbling like a man fighting his way out of the most incredible Western brawl ever devised in Hollywood. Never missing a note.

There was another standing ovation.

Elvis was panting now, gulping for air, trying to swallow more Gatorade. And grinning.

"Yesterday," he sang, "all my troubles seemed so far away. . . ." It had come full circle. Elvis, who had been the inspiration for the Beatles, now was singing a Beatles song. And then he sang a second one, "Hey Jude." Not the entire song. Just the title and the rhythm sounds ("Na na na na nanana na . . ."), over and over again. If before, the showroom resembled an orgy scene, or at least a pentecostal revival at fever pitch, now it was a giant sing-along.

As Elvis finished the next song, "Johnny B. Goode," an old Chuck Berry hit, many were calling requests. Elvis nodded his thanks but went on, diving into one of his earliest songs, "Mystery Train," which ran directly (same rhythm line) into "Tiger Man."

"I'm the king of the jungle," Elvis sang, "they call me Tiger Man. . . ."

He closed with "What'd I Say" and two thousand people were on their feet. Elvis bowed and left and came back and sang the song he intended to close with anyway, the song he has since closed every show with, "Can't Help Falling in Love."

THE PRESS CONFERENCE

The thunder continued as Elvis moved through the good wishes and glad hands backstage, heading for his dressing room to change for a press conference the Colonel had arranged.

"Why have you waited so long to perform live again?" the first reporter asked.

"We had to finish up the movie commitments we had before I could start on this. I missed the live contact with an audience. It was getting harder and harder to sing to a camera all day long."

"Will you do more live shows?"

"I sure hope so. I want to. I would like to play all over the world. Yes, Britain of course is included. I chose to play Las Vegas because it is a place people come to from all over."

"Are you tired of your present type of movie?"

"Yes, I want to change the type of script I have been doing."

"Do you feel it was a mistake to do so many movie soundtrack albums?"

"I think so. When you do ten songs in a movie, they can't all be good songs. Anyway, I got tired of singing to turtles."

It was as if the press wanted Elvis to recant. The same question kept coming at him.

"What kind of scripts would you like to do?"

"Something with meaning. I couldn't dig always playing the guy who'd get into a fight, beat the guy up, and in the next shot sing to him."

And finally the reporters moved on. "Did you enjoy performing live again?" one asked.

Elvis said he had been nervous, that he didn't feel relaxed until after "Love Me Tender." He dodged a question about his salary, looking toward the Colonel, who was wearing a long white laboratory jacket covered with the words ELVIS IN PERSON. He admitted he dyed his hair but said it was only because he'd always done it for the movies. And he joked.

"How do you like the role of being a father?"

"I like it."

"Do you plan to add to your family?"

"I'll let you know."

"How does your wife feel about you being a sex symbol again?"

"We're planning to add to our family."

THE REVIEWS

The critics were ecstatic. "Elvis Retains Touch in Return to Stage," *Billboard* headlined, pointedly placing the review on its country music page, where Elvis first appeared exactly fifteen years earlier. Said David Dalton in *Rolling Stone:* "Elvis was supernatural, his own resurrection. . . ." Ellen Willis in *The New Yorker* said that if Elvis continued to perform, and "Suspicious Minds" was as big as it should be, he again would have a significant impact on popular music. *Variety* called him a superstar, said he was "immediately affable . . . very much in command of the entire scene," while proving himself to be one of the most powerful acts in Vegas history. "There are several unbelievable things about Elvis," said *Newsweek*, "but the most incredible is his staying power in a world where meteoric careers fade like shooting stars." And on and on and on. The reviews couldn't have been better if the Colonel had written them himself.

The Fall of the King

Roy Carr and Mick Farren

Elvis's 1969 return to the stage in Las Vegas was one of the high points of his career. However, as Roy Carr and Mick Farren write in their 1982 book *Elvis Presley: The Illustrated Record*, it was soon followed by a dramatic fall. Rather than announcing a major tour, Elvis decided to do only a few shows a year. In 1973 he performed for his *Aloha from Hawaii* special—a live, internationally televised concert—but after that he became increasingly withdrawn and obsessive. He abused a variety of drugs, including amphetamines, tranquilizers, and painkillers. In 1972 he divorced his wife, Priscilla, and thereafter he alternated between bouts of extreme boredom and obsession with religion or karate. Elvis died at Graceland on August 16, 1977, apparently of overdose. Efforts to cover up his drug habits—including theft of the autopsy report— have made it impossible to know exactly what happened on the night of Elvis's death.

The obvious question was—what was Elvis going to do next? The point had been proved, he had made his comeback and he was right there in the public eye. The problem was that the momentum had to be sustained if the series of International Hotel shows were not to be simply a flash in the pan. Many observers expected that Elvis would follow through with a full scale tour of the USA, if not of the world. The single of 'Suspicious Minds' was a number one hit and had gone gold. The double album, *From Memphis to Vegas/From Vegas to Memphis* had also topped one million sales. The last of the vehicle movies, *Change of Habit* with Mary Tyler Moore, had crawled away to well deserved oblivion, and there were no more contracted. In terms of his career, Elvis was free, loose and riding high. He could do just about anything that he wanted.

It came as something of a surprise when it was announced that there would be no tour in the immediate future and instead, Elvis would return to the International Hotel for the month of January, 1970. It seemed a little soon, and some fans, confronted by the idea of Elvis playing Las Vegas twice in the same six months, wondered if once again, the same sloppy line of least resistance career direction that had embroiled Presley in nearly ten years of bad movies was once again at work. Could it be that Elvis was simply exchanging a well worn Hollywood rut for a new Las Vegas rut?

As 1970 drew closer, these fears appeared to be unfounded. Plans were drawn up for a million dollar-plus close-circuit TV concert to be held at the Las Vegas Convention Centre in August and transmitted by Filmways Concert Associates to 275 cities at $5 a ticket. Elvis would be guaranteed one million bucks. This idea was scrapped because it was decided that there was much more money to be made on the road. Subsequently, 'market tests' were carried out. First, at Houston Astrodome (February 27–March 1st), followed by six September shows (Phoenix, St. Louis, Detroit, Miami, Tampa, Mobile) and a predominantly West Coast trip of eight venues in November.

Although the Astrodome concerts turned out to be little more than freakshows, with atrocious sound and almost unbelievable distances between some sections of the crowd and the performer, Elvis walked away with $1.2 million. At the same time, it was possible to peg seat prices so the cheapest were only a dollar. This was something of a thank-you gesture to the east Texas fans whose loyalty had been so crucial in the early days of 1954–5.

Elvis was clearly back in the live action groove, and working a schedule that would have seemed tough to bands whose members were considerably younger. Through 1970 he played 137 shows. In 1971 he upped the ante and made the year's total 156, while 1972 saw 164 performances, including four triumphant concerts at New York's Madison Square Garden. It seemed as though all America wanted to see Elvis Presley and, in his turn, Elvis was doing his level best to accommodate them.

ALOHA FROM HAWAII

Beyond America, there was the rest of the world, however. After three years, Europe, Japan and Australia all started asking, quite rightly, when they were going to see some action. They had, after all, been important markets for Presley ever since the start of his career, but he had never sung a live note in any of these territories, except for some impromptu jamming during his draftee years in Germany.

Obviously something had to be done for these international fans. The solution, formulated in a deal between Parker and NBC, was hardly what the fans expected, though. The devoted millions, spread right across the planet, clearly thought that they were entitled to a full scale, Elvis Presley world tour. Instead, they were given *Aloha from Hawaii*—a live concert, from the Hawaiian International Centre Arena, would be beamed across the world via satellite. It had the potential to reach one and a half billion people, more than had watched the first moonwalk. Technology was hardly a substitute for a real live Elvis, but, for the time being, it was the best that the overseas faithful were going to get.

Adding insult to injury, there were a number of countries that declined to subscribe to the NBC space hookup. The most notable to opt out was the United Kingdom. Neither ITA nor BBC, the two British networks, were willing to buy the show and, for years to come, the home of The Beatles and The Rolling Stones had to make do with bootleg video tapes.

Once again, the world had to wait until well after Elvis' death for an explanation as to why Presley never toured anywhere but in the United States and Canada. The major coup of Albert Goldman, the author of the otherwise reprehensible biography *Elvis* (not to be confused with Jerry Hopkins' work of the same title), was in bringing to the attention of the world something that many Presleyphiles had known for years—that Colonel Tom Parker was in fact a Dutch national, an illegal immigrant called Andreas Cornelius Van Kuijk. Parker had always been characteristically cagey about his origins, vaguely claiming that he was the son of "carny folk". If Goldman is correct, the reason that he turned down millions in offers from all over the world for Elvis to appear in person was simply that Parker could not legally obtain a passport without giving away his secret. (He never once visited Elvis in Germany, but busied himself instead in repackaging back-catalogue.)

Aloha from Hawaii seems, in retrospect, to have been the final peak of Elvis' career. It was a strange and debatable peak unfortunately, that seemed, despite a killer version of 'Blue Suede Shoes' and a reading of 'This Time You Gave Me A Mountain' that didn't leave a dry eye in the house, to have more to do with megalomania than rock 'n' roll.

The Hillbilly Cat had turned into something that might have been dreamt up by Marvel Comics. In his spangled eagle cape and jewelled jumpsuit, the fifties hoodlum had been transformed into something out of science fiction—a superhero, the Handsome Dictator of the Universe. Without question, it was the most colossal one man show ever attempted by an entertainer, and also without question one of the most colossal ego trips in recent history. Sadly, Elvis would do nothing to equal it during the rest of his life.

Despite his continuing successes, even before *Aloha*, a pattern was starting to emerge. Elvis was slipping into a routine that consisted of six months' touring and two stints in the Las Vegas Hilton. It hardly boded well, for any time a regular pattern started to show up in the work of Elvis Presley the quality began to suffer. The problem that confronted Elvis Presley throughout his career was that success was never once equated with artistic achievement, but with the acquisition of the biggest bankroll. Whatever spark of inspiration Elvis displayed was quickly damped down by the production line attitude to his work. It was inevitable that Elvis got bored quicker than any other major artist, and that sooner or later the boredom would show. Elvis seemed to run on three year bursts of energy—the three years prior to the army, when he was building his reputation; the first three years of the sixties, when he still seemed interested in what he was doing; and the three years after the NBC Special.

RUMOURS ABOUND

Not only was there concern about his work, but by 1973 other rumours were starting to cloud the previously clean-cut Presley image. His wife had left him, and it seemed as though his ego was reeling. If Elvis Presley couldn't find true love, who the hell could?

A significant incident took place during Presley's 1975 stint at the Las Vegas Hilton. The Showroom was, as usual, packed and the show ended with the usual tumultuous applause. Suddenly, however, the audience was subjected to an abrupt and unexpected change of routine. Instead of sprinting for the dressing room, Elvis remained standing at the microphone. He suddenly announced that he wanted to tell it like it really was, to "set the record straight".

"The other night I had the 'flu real bad. Someone started the report that I was strung out. If I ever find out who started that, I'll knock their goddamn head off. I've never been strung out in my life".

He was like a man with an obsession. It was as though he seriously believed that the world thought of him as a hopeless drug addict. The 2,500 strong crowd watched stunned as Presley ranted on. He had never touched drugs in his life, and had no intention of starting on drugs in the future. Never was there a more perfect case of a man damning himself by protesting too much.

Over the years there had been literally hundreds of rumours about Elvis Presley—it would be unimaginable that it could be any other way. Elvis Presley was the world's greatest rock star. He simply had to be the focal point for speculation, gossip and plain, old fashioned lies, and his bouts of Garbo-like seclusion only served to intensify the talk. At least three times in his career, fictitious stories of his death spread like wild fire. "Elvis is dead" was a recurring theme long before the 1970 lunacy about the death of Paul McCartney.

Ironically, rumours of drug abuse by Presley were comparatively mild. At no point did he flaunt any kind of stoned persona comparable to those of Jimi Hendrix, Jim Morrison or Grace Slick. He was never hauled away on drugs charges like John Lennon, Brian Jones, Keith Richards or Jerry Garcia. Compared to the wild bunch of second generation rock stars, Elvis was a picture of rectitude and conservatism.

Of course, the dopeheads speculated on the kind of drugs Elvis used—the same kind of speculation that attributed an amphetamine habit to John F. Kennedy. Some reasoned that Elvis couldn't have come out of the southern rockabilly circuit without dabbling with the same amphetamines that killed Hank Williams, nearly incapacitated Johnny Cash and helped Jerry Lee Lewis turn himself into an awesome and, at times, demonic legend. Others claimed that they were certain that Elvis was stoned during some of the rehearsal sequences in the movie *Elvis: That's The Way It Is.* Still more pointed out that since, according to all the available information, Elvis didn't drink, he must be into some kind of turn-on—otherwise, what was the point of being the king of rock 'n' roll? Most sensible people dismissed the drug rumours—if they wanted to worry about Elvis Presley at all, they could fret about his broken marriage, the stories of his compulsive eating, his obesity, his deteriorating health, and his wild and bizarre spending sprees that sometimes resulted in total strangers receiving gifts of cars or expensive jewellery.

PROLONGED AND MASSIVE DRUG ABUSE

It was only after Presley's death that the frightening truth about the real extent of his prolonged and massive drug abuse became public knowledge. Sadly for everyone concerned, it was the hippie theorists who were right and the sensible people who were wrong. Not even the hippies, though, had suspected the degree of crazed disregard with which Elvis could swallow almost every variety of pill.

The controversies over Presley's death and drug habits are unlikely to be satisfactorily resolved, if for no other reason than that too many of his fans would prefer their idol laid to rest with an unsullied memory. (Indeed, many still believe the drug stories to be simply a smear campaign.) All reliable information does, however, point to the fact that Presley could (and did) consume drugs in such quantity and variety that he made Keith Richards and Jimi Hendrix look like boy scouts.

Perversely, Presley's drug abuse was strictly confined to prescription stimulants and narcotics. This may have been because he liked to maintain the pretence that he was only taking pills for his health, or could have been a natural precaution against the possibility of arrest (although it would have taken a courageous 'narc' to actually bust Elvis Presley). If exclusively using prescription drugs was an act of caution, once the prescription was handed to the druggist, all caution ceased. Bodyguard Red West recalled in the book "Elvis: What Happened", published before Elvis' death, "He takes pills to go to sleep, he takes pills to get up. He takes pills to go to the john and he takes pills to stop him going to the john. There have been times where he was so hyper on uppers that he had trouble breathing, and on one occasion he thought that he was going to die. His system doesn't work anymore like a normal human being's. The pills do all the work for him. He is a walking pharmaceutical shop".

Stories conflict as to when, where and how Elvis' drug habits got their start. Some stories claim that it was as early as his first days of touring with Scotty Moore and Bill Black and hanging out at Sun Records. A less than kind version of these stories was that he would even rip-off his mother's diet pills in order to get sufficiently wired to overcome his chronic shyness and to face an audience.

Red West, on the other hand, denies that Presley took drugs during those early years, and claims that he was "high enough on his natural energy". According to West, Elvis' first dabblings came during his army stint in Germany, when he was given dexedrine by an overzealous and less than scrupulous sergeant who liked to keep his men snappy and alert during all-night manoeuvres.

Whatever the origins of Presley's drug use, most sources agree that he was pretty much a full blown speed freak, using all kinds of amphetamines and similar uppers during the long haul in the sixties when he turned out one idiot movie after another.

Elvis, however, appeared to thrive on the speed diet. "In the early days the man had a tremendous constitution. He would never stop".—Red West. The main problem seemed to have been to keep him amused. His work demanded so little of his talent that there was a constant need for diversion; a need that almost certainly gave rise to Presley's almost pathological promiscuity, the various excesses with guns, cars and other expensive (and sometimes dangerous) toys.

It was only in the seventies, when he had returned to the live stage, that he began switching to tranquillisers and downers and using valium, quaaludes and more powerful pain killers like percodan, demerol and dilaudid (which is normally only prescribed to terminal cancer patients). Obviously much of this downer use was a result of the return to a far more demanding way of life. Touring and playing live shows required more concentration and stamina than the comparatively easy routine of movie work. Elvis needed to regularly relax, and the downers initially provided a source of instant relaxation. They also, however, brought with them a set of unfortunate and destructive side effects, and much of Presley's mental and physical deterioration in the seventies must have been due to his overkill drug abuse.

Apart from the need to relax there is little doubt that Elvis was well into the recreational side of drug abuse. As early as

1971, Elvis and an unnamed girl fan came close to overdosing after a night of lovemaking and getting high on massive amounts of the cough medicine Hycadan. It is just about possible, in the case of, say, a Jimi Hendrix or a Charlie Parker, if not to condone, at least to ignore an artist's drug habits, so long as his work does not suffer. In the case of Elvis Presley, the drugs appear to have taken over so completely that, toward the end, Presley seemed incapable of doing anything but going through the motions in front of a totally loyal crowd.

The Elvis Presley business operation proved itself far better at cover up than creativity. The world at large heard virtually nothing about Elvis' drug related problems. Even when he was hospitalised on a number of occasions, the fans worried about glaucoma or cancer, obesity and recurrent respiratory complaints. Nobody suspected that Presley had actually OD'ed a number of times, on one occasion only surviving because his father administered artificial respiration.

THE DISINTEGRATION OF ELVIS PRESLEY

The disintegration of Elvis Presley clearly starts in earnest after the split with Priscilla in 1972 and the subsequent divorce one year later. No amount of PR work could cover the fact that Presley had suffered a major emotional wound, the only debatable point being whether it was to his heart or to his ego. Aside from his drug taking going into high gear, he also began to show symptoms of full blown megalomania. He became obsessed with uniforms and insignia, even managing to finagle the personal presentation to him of an honorary federal narcotics agent badge by the then President, Richard Nixon.

His behaviour became increasingly erratic and strange. He suffered bouts of irrational, hysterical temper. He went on chronic eating binges, and tried for a while to order a mafia-style hit on Mike Stone, the karate instructor with whom Priscilla had run away. At the same time, he became almost psychotic over the possibility of an attempt on his own life.

When, with Elvis dead, most of his one time entourage had no more reason to keep quiet, the flood gates of rumour were opened wide. At first the problem seemed to be one of chronic boredom. He had once confided to a musician friend that he had no competition left on Earth, there was nothing left to prove. As far as Elvis was concerned, no other performer could challenge him or eclipse his popularity.

Boredom, however, escalated to what can only be described as full scale mental problems. His Dracula-style day (which began at sunset), prompted actress girlfriend Linda Thompson, who lived with him for the majority of the time between his divorce and his death, to comment that "life with Elvis meant living like a bat". He seemed to start seeing himself as some sort of messiah, believing that his shows were not so much entertainment as holy events, during which he could commune with his disciples and they, in turn, could worship him. Religion apparently took hold of him, and he had bouts of reading the Bible to his hangers-on. At extreme moments, he even suffered from delusions that he could heal the sick, and control the weather, by an effort of will.

Even his much vaunted karate seems to have been a myth fostered by the ever present flatterers. Sonny West describes how Elvis turned up at a karate studio—in a heat wave—festooned with jewels and gold, a designer karate suit, a large flashy overcoat and, just to top off the ensemble, an eastern style turban. He was blocked out of his mind and very out of condition. On this and other occasions, the opponents would let him win, and allow him to go on believing that he could whip all comers. In fact, most of the time, the downers made his co-ordination so bad that he was as much a danger to himself as to his sparring partner.

There were even darker rumours—that he would indulge in racist outbursts, and exhibit a level of bigotry that he normally suppressed in public. He was also gun happy, and even in his most relaxed moments (and on stage!) was prone to be armed to the teeth. Gabe Tucker, a Parker employee, and one of the many of Presley's outer circle who rushed into print with a ghosted collection of reminiscences, provides a gauge to the degree of Presley's mania in his book *Up and Down with Elvis*. One morning the Ferrari Elvis owned failed to turn over when he pressed the starter; he walked to the trunk of the car, took out the two pistols he kept there and emptied them into the recalcitrant automobile. Once he was satisfied the car was quite dead, he growled at one of his aids to have it hauled away.

One of his companions sadly asked him, "Why did you do that?"

"I got pressures, man", Elvis mumbled. "I have a demanding family, an expensive life, and I'm lonesome".

The worst occasions of all were when the chemical cocktails in his system would push him well beyond the danger point. He would lose all physical control and fall without warning into deep stupors. He would even lose control of his bowels. Linda Thompson only moved out from Graceland a few months before his death because she could no longer handle his epic drug taking.

"His death could have happened any number of times during the years I spent with him. When a person knocks himself out each night with sleeping pills, he is just as apt to fall asleep face down on the floor as he is to be safely tucked away in bed when the medication hits. For that reason, Elvis required an unfathomable amount of attention. Elvis had a self-destructive vein, and I couldn't watch him self-destruct".

ELVIS'S DEATH

The worst irony of all is that, as far as anyone could tell, the night that Elvis died was only a "normal" night in the Memphis mansion. Even in a normal night though, Elvis had, according to his step brother Mickey Stanley, been brought sixteen pills, a mixture of valium, quaaludes and barbiturates.

Ironically, there is some reason to suppose that, in the last few months of his life, Elvis may have been making some sort of effort to straighten himself out. Some reports claim that he had attempted a drug rehabilitation course at the Hazelden Foundation, Center City, Minnesota. He had even attempted to enlist the help of Dorsey Burnette (brother of Johnny Burnette), who had given up a life of casual booze, sex and drugs when he had become a born again Christian. Burnette had promised to visit Presley, but by the time he made that visit, Presley was on his way to the morgue. Other stories tell of Presley's intention to make the bi-centennial tour his farewell, and how he was confident that retirement would bring back Priscilla and his daughter. Tragically, if these attempts were made, they all came to nothing.

In the first few hours after Elvis had been discovered dead on the bathroom floor, it would seem that some kind of cover-up had already started. Independent investigators, including Geraldo Rivera of ABC Network News, make the charge that the Presley retainers conspired with Shelby County, Tennessee, health officials to conceal the fact that Elvis had OD'ed. Their motive seemed to be that, if the Presley image was tarnished by the scandal of his drug habits, it would not only destroy the legend, but could also hurt Memphis' lucrative Elvis-based tourist trade. Accordingly, County Medical Examiner Jerry Francisco issued the story that Presley had died from a massive heart attack. Dr. Eric Muirhead, Chief of Pathology at the Baptist Memorial Hospital in Memphis, and Dr. Noel Floredo, who attended the autopsy on Presley, both attribute the man's death to "uppers, downers and pain killing drugs . . . most probably an interaction of several drugs".

The situation will never be satisfactorily resolved. All notes, reports and photographs of the death scene and the autopsy are missing, and the contents of Presley's stomach had been destroyed without any attempt at analysis. In lieu of hard evidence, the findings by a medical board that George ('Dr. Nick') Nichopolous, the resident doctor at the Presley court, was guilty of grossly overprescribing dangerous drugs to nineteen patients, including Elvis Presley and Jerry Lee Lewis, would indicate that the weight of medical opinion favours the theory that Elvis Presley died of an overdose. Indeed, between January and August 1977, Nichopolous had prescribed some 5,300 pills, mainly amphetamines, quaaludes, tuinol, nembutal, codine, phenobarbitol and dilaudid to Elvis Presley. In the fall of 1981, Dr. Nick was put on trial in Memphis, but was acquitted when the jury found no evidence of malicious intent.

It is, however, all too easy to make someone like Nichopolous the scapegoat for Presley's death. At worst he can only be regarded as an accomplice or accessory to the rock star's self-destruction. Nobody forced Presley to take absurd quantities of drugs. The worst that was done to him was that nobody ever had the courage to point out what he was doing to himself and tell him to stop but, as Graceland's aide David Stanley put it:

"Nobody ever said no to Elvis Presley".

The morning after his death, the 17th of August, 1977, Elvis Presley lay in state, while 25,000 mourners filed past the solid brass casket. He was dressed in a white suit, light blue shirt and a darker blue tie. The next day, the funeral started at 2 P.M. Rex Humbard, the nationally known TV evangelist from Akron, Ohio, conducted the service. It was a private funeral—Jackie Kahane, the comedian who had been opening Presley's shows, gave the eulogy, and Kathy Westmoreland, one of his back-up singers, sang two gospel songs. The pallbearers were Charlie Hodge, Joe Esposito, George Klein, Lamar Fike, Felton Jarvis and George Nichopolous.

The death of Elvis Presley produced a multitude of reactions. Obviously there was an enormous amount of genuine pain and grief, but there was also a tinge of craziness and a lot of eyes on a fast buck. One Hollywood cynic exclaimed "great career move" when he heard the news. Of the crowds that gathered on Elvis Presley Boulevard in Memphis in the days that immediately followed August 16th 1977, and the 1½ million who would visit his grave in the first year, by far the greatest percentage had come to pay genuine respect to an idol, a hero, a man who had become so much a part of some lives that he was thought of as a friend.

CHAPTER 5

Long Live the King

The Wide World of Elvis Fandom

Peter Harry Brown and Pat H. Broeske

After his death, explain Elvis biographers Peter Harry Brown and Pat H. Broeske, fans took a renewed interest in Elvis Presley. Today Elvis Presley Enterprises, a division of his estate, earns millions of dollars from the sale of not only Elvis's records but also the countless knickknacks and memorabilia that bear his image. Hundreds of thousands of fans visit Graceland each year. An estimated 2,000 entertainers perform as Elvis imitators, who dress like Elvis and perform his songs in homage to the King of Rock and Roll. Elvis's most devoted followers hold him in almost religious awe, and some have even claimed that he is still alive. Decades after his death, "Elvis mania" survives.

He may be gone, but he is far from forgotten. Elvis Presley refuses to leave the building. He lives on in recordings, merchandising, books, films, and the collective conscience.

GRACELAND

Some seven hundred thousand visitors annually make the trek to Graceland, which opened as a tourist attraction in 1982 and ranks as the second most-visited house in the country, following the White House. Though the audio tour delivers a sanitized depiction of Elvis's life and times, complete with girlish exclamations by Priscilla Presley about how much fun they used to have there, the house and grounds have retained the sense of sanctuary that was integral to Presley's pressured life.

For Elvis, Graceland is sanctuary still. He lies out beyond the swimming pool—alongside his mother, father, and Grandma Minnie Mae.

Though Elvis Presley Enterprises does not discuss monetary figures, in 1994 it was reported that the Presley estate was a $100-million-a-year industry of music, movies, and memorabilia. Much of that memorabilia was doubtless purchased at the sprawling shopping complex located directly across the street from Graceland, which operates the shops and maintains a close vigil over the licensing of merchandise.

It has been largely due to the wakefulness of Priscilla Presley—who reinvented herself as a tough and shrewd businesswoman—and her attorneys that her ex-husband's estate was turned into a monstrous moneymaker. Following Presley's death, and the scrutinizing of his financial status, Colonel Tom Parker was sued on behalf of Lisa Marie for fraud and mismanagement. A Memphis court went on to rule that Parker—who had taken between twenty-five and fifty percent of Presley's income, and who was then involved in his own Elvis licensing ventures—had no legal rights to the Presley estate.

Following additional lawsuits that accused him of having taken financial advantage of Presley, Parker sold his Presley master recordings to RCA for $2 million. It has been said that he also sold his silence. For Elvis Presley Enterprises acquired his paperwork about his extraordinary relationship with Presley.

In the meantime, Presley's sole heir has become a kitsch celebrity in her own right—the result of Lisa Marie's 1994 Dominican Republic wedding to pop superstar Michael Jackson.

But there are no photographs of Lisa Marie and Michael—whom she has since divorced—at Graceland, or in the adjoining shops. Nor are there any photographs of the troubled, bloated Elvis. Word is that the images on display are "holding" at 170 pounds.

OTHER SITES

Elsewhere beyond Graceland, there are plenty of celebrations of Elvis Presley the man, complete with flaws. As Sam Phillips, the man who discovered him, reminds, "Even when he was in horrible shape, emotionally and physically, Elvis always conveyed a real caring."

The tiny, restored Sun Records in Memphis offers a surprisingly affecting tour of the single room where a nineteen-year-old truck driver made his earliest recordings.

In Tupelo, Mississippi, a dollar buys a ticket into the shotgun shack where Elvis was born. It's just a short drive from the antiquated-looking Tupelo Hardware, "the store where Elvis bought his first guitar." That's what it used to say on a $1.50 key ring sold by the store, until lawyers from Elvis Presley Enterprises threatened legal action. The store's guitar-shaped key ring now reads, "Where Gladys bought her son his first guitar." For collectors of Presley memorabilia, it may be the best bargain of all.

And for a heartfelt tour, it would be hard to top Graceland Too—located in Holly Springs, Mississippi (between Tupelo and Memphis). The home of Paul MacLeod and his son, Elvis Aaron Presley MacLeod, is a virtual shrine to Elvis, open twenty-four hours. Repeat visitors get to be photographed in a special black leather jacket and have their picture showcased alongside those of thousands of other True Believers. Call it Roadside Elvis.

There have been tributes in song (including Paul Simon's "Graceland"), fiction (such as Alice Walker's short story "Nineteen Fifty-Five"), art (there are myriad Presley-inspired exhibitions), as well as in a twenty-nine-cent postage stamp. And if imitation is the sincerest form of flattery, there are always impersonators—of every nationality.

STUDYING ELVIS

For serious students of Elvismania, there are now college courses and lectures dissecting his impact on society, on culture, on religion, and more. For several years, the prestigious University of Mississippi made headlines with its scholarly summer conference on the significance of Elvis Presley. Vernon Chadwick, founder and director of the conference, who also taught the country's first university courses on Elvis, hails Presley as "a rebellious, radicalizing force of democracy, equal opportunity, and free expression."

And lest anyone forget his generosities—to literally countless charities and causes—there are more than five hundred fan clubs worldwide whose members are known for their tireless efforts on behalf of various charities. As Elvis used to say, being generous "is like throwin' a stone in a pond. It ripples out."

Presley also reached out to fans in a way no star has done before, or since.

Has any star ever posed for more candid photographs? Signed more autograph books? To the consternation of his buddies, Elvis used to insist on climbing out of his limo—as they were about to leave one arena and head for the next gig—to race over for a Kodak moment. When his friends

INSIDE GRACELAND

In his book The Boy Who Dared to Rock: The Definitive Elvis, *Paul Lichter describes Graceland as it appeared when Elvis first purchased the estate in 1957.*

The two-story stone house is a classic example of southern architecture. Upon entering through the famed sculptured gates, you found yourself traveling along a three-quarter-mile curved driveway bordered by well-tended lawns that swept by majestically. The house was surrounded by perfectly manicured trees. In the evening, pale blue lights illuminated the driveway and reflected off the house's exterior. The carport, located in the rear of Graceland, housed Elvis' many cars, motorcycles, and three-wheeled go-carts. A short distance from the house were an office building and a kennel for his many pets. The flagstone patio featured a giant television, guitars, drums, and furniture. From the patio you descended the flagstone steps to the first level of the terrace, where you found a fireplace and kidney-shaped swimming pool. At either side of the terrace were tall white pillars. The entire area was housed in pink and yellow fiberglass, and in the evening the lights gave off a rainbow glow that was an unbelievable visual experience.

The lower level of the house was completely covered in a thick white carpet. The den and game room could be found here. The walls were of softly burnished oak, almost every inch covered with the awards of a fantastic career. The main floor consisted of a music room (in this room were over 25,000 record albums, part of Elvis' fabulous collection), living and dining rooms, and the kitchen and the maids' quarters. Vernon and Gladys' rooms were on the second floor, but in later years all of the rooms had been converted for Elvis' use. Elvis had a bedroom–sitting room, bathroom, and dressing room equipped with a barber salon. A private conference room was designed by Elvis and contained a large oval oak table.

Elvis may have come from humble beginnings, but at his peak the King lived in a palace.

Paul Lichter, *The Boy Who Dared to Rock: The Definitive Elvis.* Garden City, NJ: Dolphin Books, 1978.

protested, Elvis said, "It's only because of them that we're here in the first place."

Of course, the music made it all happen in the first place. In that arena, Elvis truly is the King. In a feat unsurpassed in music history, he has sold more than 1 billion records worldwide.

ELVIS SIGHTINGS

In his lifetime, Elvis was constantly reinventing himself. The same holds true in death.

According to the *Los Angeles Times,* Nobel laureate Kary Mullis has obtained the rights to extract DNA from Presley's hair, for the manufacture of jewelry. The story was headlined: "A Hunk of Burnin' Love on a Chain."

And of course there are the sightings. The 1988 paperback curiosity *Is Elvis Alive?* by Gail Brewer-Giorgio contributed to the mania by raising questions about Presley's "death," and underlining assorted oddities regarding Presley. Example: *lives* is an anagram for *Elvis.*

Weekly World News, the supermarket tabloid known for its revelations about the "Bat Boy" and Bigfoot, regularly charts Presley's whereabouts, with some assistance from a Michigan housewife who has spotted Elvis twice—once at a Kalamazoo Burger King, another time at a Vicksburg convenience store. The tabloid somehow also listened in on "secret" White House tapes, proving that Presley telephoned President Clinton. He also reportedly continues to dispense advice to his daughter: "Elvis Tells Lisa Marie, 'Divorce Michael.'"

Ironically, *Weekly World News* is a sister publication of the *National Enquirer*—which took and owns the famed Presley coffin photo—whose editors steadfastly maintain that the star is dead.

Yet among those who maintain that Presley is dead and buried are those who insist that his spirit literally lives on. Examples abound in a recent book by a "psychic investigator," who revealed Presley's messages from beyond the grave. Among other things, the star's ghost helped a worried father locate his runaway son.

ELVIS'S LEGENDARY GENEROSITY

Still others—especially associates and fans—work through the fan clubs and various Elvis "conventions" to promote another kind of spirit: Elvis's own good nature. Mike McGregor, a lanky Mississippian who tended to Elvis's horses, and went on to make some of his jewelry, was in the Graceland guard gate the night a car bearing Louisiana plates pulled up. "They handed me a note that they wanted to get to Elvis," said Mc-Gregor. In it was a heartfelt thank-you from a boy's club which had been robbed of its kitchen supplies. Elvis had read a "teensy article" about the theft in the local paper, and had promptly sent off a check to cover the loss.

"When people talk to me about Elvis, I like to remind them that in addition to being the biggest star ever, he also had the biggest heart ever," says McGregor.

Don Wilson knows firsthand about that heart. He was just ten years old, and suffering the recent deaths of his parents and sister—as the result of a train crash—when his grandmother took him to see Elvis at the Houston Astrodome in 1971.

Wilson got to meet Elvis backstage. Later, unbeknownst to him, his grandmother sent a letter to Elvis, telling him about what had happened. To Don's surprise, Elvis later sent him a card expressing his condolences. It marked the beginning of a six-year "friendship" by correspondence, during which time Wilson received notes, albums, and even pieces of clothing. Wilson went on to visit Elvis at Graceland.

"What can I tell you? It literally changed my life to think that Elvis Presley cared about me," said Wilson, who is today a songwriter, disc jockey and also—and appropriately—an Elvis impersonator. He goes by the moniker "The Great Don El."

THE CONTINUING FASCINATION

As to why it all happened to Elvis—out of everyone in the world—Carl Perkins, the rockabilly legend who wrote "Blue Suede Shoes," surmises that it was fated. "I've come to believe that when Elvis was born, God said, 'Here is the messenger, and I'm going to make him the best-looking guy, and I'm going to give him every piece of rhythm he needs to move that good-looking body on that stage.'" Mused Perkins, "I was fighting a battle working with him, knowing that I looked like Mr. Ed, that mule, and here was a guy that could go out and clear his throat and have ten thousand people scream."

Bob Dylan has called Presley "the deity supreme of rock-'n'-roll religion as it exists in today's form." For Dylan, "hearing him for the first time was like busting out of jail."

To Bruce Springsteen, "it's like he came along and whispered a dream in everybody's ear, and then we all dreamed it somehow."

Rolling Stone's Dave Marsh once surmised, "Elvis was the King of rock and roll because he was the embodiment of its sins and virtues: grand and vulgar, rude and eloquent, powerful and frustrated, absurdly simple and awesomely complex."

As Sam Phillips put it, "I think a little mystery will always remain."

The King Remembered as a Saint

James Miller

Rock journalist James Miller notes that even before Elvis died, many of his fans regarded him with an almost religious reverence. The idolization of Elvis as a saint accelerated after his death, as fans chose to ignore the emerging details of Elvis's drug abuse and instead remember only the brighter moments in his career and the best aspects of his personality. Eventually a cult of enthusiastic fans evolved around Elvis. Miller suggests that this cult is evidence of the degree to which music, particularly rock and roll, has replaced religion as Americans' primary spiritual outlet. Elvis had the power to spiritually uplift fans with his music, and many of them have deified him for it. Miller is the editor of *The Rolling Stone Illustrated History of Rock and Roll* and the author of *Flowers in the Dustbin: The Rise of Rock and Roll, 1947–1977,* from which the following is excerpted.

The news broke in the afternoon of August 16, 1977. Elvis Aron Presley, universally recognized as the King of Rock and Roll, was dead at the age of forty-two. To a lot of people, it seemed impossible. Presley had been the idol of a still youthful generation. Like a hero of Greek mythology, he belonged to a world apart. It was perhaps a delusion spawned by the mass media, but his fame seemed immortal—and his death therefore unimaginable.

Details at first were sketchy. After being found unconscious at his Graceland mansion in Memphis, Presley had been taken by ambulance to Baptist Memorial Hospital. He was declared dead at 3:30 P.M., after efforts to revive him failed. Later that evening, a local medical examiner met with reporters and announced that Presley had died of "cardiac arrhythmia"—in other words, his heart had stopped beating. There was no evidence of any other disease, he said. And, he added, contradicting a rumor that had started to spread, Elvis Presley did not die of drug abuse.

That night, two of America's national television networks broadcast special reports. On ABC, the show's host, Geraldo Rivera, expressed relief that Elvis at least "had not followed in the melancholy rock 'n' roll tradition of Janis Joplin, Jim Morrison, Jimi Hendrix." On NBC, by contrast, David Brinkley, the moderator, explicitly broached the possibility that Elvis had in fact died of drug abuse, no matter what the examiner in Memphis was saying.

One of Brinkley's guests that evening was Steve Dunleavy. A pugnacious tabloid journalist, Dunleavy had just published a lurid little book entitled *Elvis: What Happened?*, written in collaboration with three disgruntled former Presley employees, Red West, Sonny West, and Dave Hebler. Seizing the chance to publicize their book, Dunleavy retailed for Brinkley some of the book's revelations about "the dark side of the brightest star in the world": for example, Presley's fondness for fooling around with women half his age; his streak of paranoia that sometimes issued in outbursts of reckless gunplay; and his uncontrollable appetite for a vast array of different prescription drugs—uppers, downers, powerful painkilling narcotics.

MORE THAN AN ORDINARY HUMAN BEING

But perhaps the most mind-boggling thing in Dunleavy's best-selling exposé, the first of many devoted to Presley and his private life, was the evidence it offered, not of Presley's lust for girls, guns, and pills, but rather of his apparently earnest belief in his own supernatural powers. "While the rest of the world recognizes that Elvis Aron Presley is something more than an ordinary human being, the one person who believes that most passionately is Presley himself," wrote Dunleavy, summarizing some of the gossip he had been fed. "He is addicted to the study of the Bible"—a strange thing to label an addiction! He was also "addicted," Dunleavy asserted, to "mystical religion, numerology, psychic phenomena, and the belief in life after death. He believes that he has the strength of will to move clouds in the air, and he is also convinced that there are beings on other planets. He firmly believes he is a prophet who was destined to lead, designated by God for a special role in life."

A great many of Presley's fans, certainly, regarded him with a reverence more befitting a prophet than a mere entertainer. By dusk on the night of August 16, a large and growing crowd of fans had formed outside Graceland to share their prayers and pay their final respects. Meanwhile, reporters with cameras and klieg lights roamed the scene and police struggled to maintain order.

Among a great many Americans of a certain age, a strange and confusing set of sentiments had been stirred up. "So that was his end," the writer Nick Tosches has recalled: "I was nonplussed. I had not known Elvis Presley as a man. I had never even met him. I started then to realize that, on some level of faint illogic, I had never truly thought of him as a creature of flesh and blood but rather as an absurd effulgence of hoi polloi mythology, an all-American demigod who dwelt, enthroned between Superman and the Lone Ranger, in the blue heaven of the popular imagination.". . .

DRUG ADDICT OR SAINT?

As time passed, more and more sordid details began to emerge about the true wages of Presley's immense fame. In the fall of 1979, the ABC television network broadcast a widely watched special report on Presley's death. Two years later, Albert Goldman published a scurrilous, best-selling biography.

What emerged was the picture of an infantilized sovereign, living a life of indescribable freedom and incredible luxury, innocent of lofty ambitions, drunk on his own crazy fountain of youth, heedless of conventional limits, able to satisfy virtually any passing impulse on whim, even able, if he chose, to blot out the everyday aches and pains of ordinary existence. Presley, it turned out, was a drug addict of epic proportions. In the seven and a half months leading up to his death in August of 1977, records showed that one Memphis doctor, George C. Nichopoulos, had prescribed him 1,790 amphetamines, 4,996 sedatives, and 2,019 narcotics. A blood sample drawn at the autopsy after Presley's death indicated that the singer had consumed a banquet of pills that beggared belief. Analysis revealed toxic levels of Quaalude and near-toxic levels of Codeine, Valium, and Placidyl, not to mention traces of Valmid, Pentobarbital, Butabarbital, and Phenobarbital—a lethal cocktail of sedatives and narcotics. . . .

Yet at exactly the same time, the dead singer was un-
dergoing an altogether different, superficially unrelated

NEITHER A FAILURE NOR A SAVIOR

*In the introduction to his biography of Elvis, Dave
Marsh argues that simplified accounts of Elvis's life—
both those that dismiss him as a failure and those that laud
him as a saint—diminish Elvis by reducing his complexity. Instead of propagating myths about him, Marsh believes audiences should try to understand how Elvis was able to achieve
all that he did.*

No one myth is large enough to contain Elvis. There are several, each containing many contradictory features, although
they can be boiled down into two contrary versions. One contends that Elvis was a failure. He left Sam Phillips, Memphis
and the South, Sun Records and rockabilly—his home and
place in the world—for Col. Tom Parker, Nashville, Las Vegas,
New York and Hollywood, the Army, RCA Victor, a life of
hookers, pills and dissolution. In this version, each step Elvis
took was a descent, his career an arc of unrelieved disaster.

The second basic Elvis myth insists that he was a savior. In
1981, with Elvis but four years in the grave, Sam Phillips, one
of his discoverers, stood at a podium in Memphis and vowed
that Elvis Presley was a modern-day version of Jesus Christ.
Phillips was merely adding credibility to the attitude Elvis'
hard-core followers have adopted since his death, an attitude
summed up in the posthumous slogan ELVIS LOVED YOU. It is
as if his fabled love made all the excuses necessary, not only
for Presley but for everyone—as if the Elvis story were nothing but transcendence and triumph. . . .

Why are these oversimplified versions of Elvis so widespread
and so widely accepted? Because they're needed. Some people
want to believe Elvis a failure because admitting the magnitude
of his success would make their own shortcomings unbearable.
Others want to see Elvis as a king, some kind of savior, because
granting him such stature places him outside the common
realm, beyond criticism but also beyond emulation. Either way,
those who hold these simplistic views are exempt from having
to live up to the great challenge lives such as Elvis Presley's
present to us: the challenge of seizing the chance to invent ourselves and, in the process, reinvent the world.

Dave Marsh, *Elvis.* New York: Thunder's Mouth, 1992.

metamorphosis, emerging—amazingly enough—as some kind of saint in the minds of countless enthusiasts. For every story about Elvis as a drug-addled slob, there were dozens more that seemed to demonstrate his undying love for his mother, his kindness to strangers, his acts of unstinting charity.

ELVIS WEEK

Moved no doubt by their memories of the "good" Elvis, five people gathered outside Graceland on the evening of August 15, 1978, to mark the first anniversary of Elvis's last, dark night of the soul. According to the lore that has grown up since, each one solemnly lit a candle and placed it on top of the stone wall that borders the front of Graceland. Throughout the night, the five kept vigil. So began what today is called Elvis Week— a ritualized outpouring of reverent affection for the fallen idol.

Every August, tens of thousands of pilgrims converge on Memphis, to tour Presley's mansion, to visit the Meditation Garden, to gawk at Elvis imitators, to visit museums and galleries, to attend a memorial service, to buy trinkets and souvenirs. But the most dramatic moment always comes at sundown on August 15. The simple vigil of 1978 has been turned into an annual procession up the hill to the grave site, where mourners bearing candles briefly commune with the dead man's living spirit.

While they wait their turn, the pilgrims can read the latest messages and prayers inscribed in Magic Marker and paint on the outer stone wall of Graceland:

ELVIS LIVES IN US
ELVIS, YOU ARE MY BRIDGE OVER TROUBLED WATERS
I DID DRUGS WITH ELVIS
THERE IS ONLY ONE KING AND WE KNOW WHO HE IS
ELVIS IS LOVE
ELVIS DIDN'T DESERVE TO BE WHITE
ELVIS, IT TOOK 20 YEARS TO GET HERE. NEXT STOP, HEAVEN.

The graffiti (which is periodically scrubbed clean so that new visitors can join the conversation) suggests that something more than a hobby is at issue. For many participants, Elvis Week has obviously become a quasi-religious occasion. The Meditation Garden is an American Lourdes, a place where miracles sometimes happen. Every year on August 15, the sick and the lame hobble up the hill, full of hope. As every one of the faithful well knows, on the first anniversary of Presley's death, a fan aimed his camera skyward and photographed a cumulus cloud forming a familiar profile, right down to the famous pompadour. Elvis is watching over them.

Addressing co-religionists in a letter printed in an Elvis fan club publication, an enthusiast from Belgium put it this way: "Dear friends, our LOVE and RESPECT for Elvis are unlimited . . . and we are in touch in full appreciation of our personal battle to do the best for Elvis. . . . Let's continue to work hard for him, because his LIGHT on our world today is the guarantee to give HOPE and PEACE for the next generations. . . . *We believe in Elvis just like we believe in GOD* . . . and I'm sure that we are on the right way."

Presley might have thought so, too. On more than one occasion, he expressed his own hunch that he was someone blessed with divine powers. "I don't mean to sound sacrilegious," George Klein, a Memphis disc jockey, longtime Presley crony, and media factotum remarked ten years after his death, "but he was Jesus-like. One time, when we were on the road, Elvis stopped the car. 'See that cloud,' he said. 'I'm going to move that cloud.' And the cloud moved. Maybe the wind blew it, I don't know. Elvis just looked at us and smiled."

MUSIC AS A SUBSTITUTE FOR RELIGION

The cult of Elvis poses perhaps the ultimate riddle of rock and roll. How could such a simple and sometimes nihilistic type of music strike such a deep and essentially religious chord among so many listeners?

Perhaps the answer lies outside rock and roll as a cultural form. Perhaps the cult of Elvis, like the cult of Jim Morrison, is best understood as the latest chapter in a much older story: the emergence of music in the modernizing West as a substitute for religion. In an elegant essay, the historian H.G. Koenigsberger has surveyed "the rise of music to a quasi-religious status and cult, as a psychological compensation for the decline of all forms of traditional religion." Feared by the medieval church and also by puritan reformers for its potentially wayward effects on the soul, music gradually came to be seen in the West as the most divine of art forms, and a fitting medium for the worship of God. Once the Promethean rebels of the early nineteenth century had severed music from its liturgical moorings, a path was cleared for the deification of music and the musician. "Here the gods are at work," said Goethe of Beethoven, expressing sentiments obviously shared by more than one Elvis Presley fan. "Just as Christianity arose in the international civilization of the Roman Empire," Wagner declared two generations later, "so music emerges out of the chaos of modern civilization. Both proclaim: 'Our kingdom is not of this world.'"

In 1957, at a time when Elvis Presley was still a young man and superficially on top of "this world," he expressed a telling ambivalence about the immensity of his worldly fame and the enormity of the carnal passions he had so visibly provoked, perhaps because he had not entirely purged himself of the old puritan distrust of music and its potential for exciting errant raptures. After Easter services that year, Presley approached the pastor at his church. According to someone who overheard their conversation, "He said, 'Pastor, I am the most miserable young man you have ever seen. I have got more money than I can ever spend. I have thousands of fans out there, and I have a lot of people who call themselves my friends, but I am miserable. I am not doing a lot of things that you have taught me, and I am doing some things that you taught me not to do.'"

He struck a similar tone of anxious bewilderment in comments to a reporter he made at roughly the same time. "I never expected to be anyone important," the twenty-two-year-old rock star said. "Maybe I'm not now, but whatever I am, whatever I will become will be what God has chosen for me.

"Some people I know can't figure out how Elvis Presley happened. I don't blame them for wondering that. Sometimes I wonder myself."

It is something like this sense of wonder at the marvelous creative abilities of a simple country boy, tinged with awe at the reckless power of that boy's imagination and appetites running wild, that Elvis Aron Presley evidently managed to convey to millions of people round the world. And it was a similar sort of wonder, at the essentially mysterious power of a song with a big beat, even the simplest of songs, to uplift and transfigure the soul, that surely helped fuel the rise to global prominence of rock and roll, from Elvis to the Beatles and beyond.

THE WORLD TURNED UPSIDE DOWN

If the desires and yearnings nourished by that cultural form were as often as not puerile and self-destructive, just like those that Presley, at the end of his life, indulged without inhibition or limit, a transcendental aura still surrounds him, as it surrounds every other avatar of excess consecrated by the rock culture industry, from Jim Morrison and Sid Vicious and Kurt Cobain to rappers like Tupac Shakur and the Notorious B.I.G., both gunned down in the 1990s.

In the world turned upside down by Elvis Presley, it was as if the sinners had become saints, ignorance had become bliss, and the freedom of a child at play was the very image of true happiness. Even better, the feeling of bliss conveyed by the music, like the image of freedom the idol embodied, could be bought and sold and shared. For the faithful—the young and the forever young at heart—attendance at concerts and the collecting of recordings functioned as sacraments, the key elements in a novel kind of consumer religion.

To an outsider, the kind of cults that have formed around Elvis Presley and the Beatles and Bob Dylan and Jim Morrison and Ziggy Stardust and Bruce Springsteen may well seem absurd. But such was the regime founded by the King of Rock and Roll—the once and future Messiah of a new cultural form.

Elvis's Lasting Impact on U.S. Culture

Gilbert B. Rodman

Rock and roll existed before Elvis became popular. However, Gilbert B. Rodman asserts that Elvis was directly responsible for the social revolution (or cultural formation, as Rodman calls it) that is often associated with rock and roll. The music Elvis sang, the way he performed on stage, and even the way he dressed all challenged prevailing social norms. Moreover, the fact such a young, seemingly normal person could become so incredibly famous inspired an entire generation to strive to achieve more in their lives—to "dream bigger dreams"—than most of their parents would have thought possible. Rodman concludes that, because of Elvis, rock and roll inspired mainstream America to question the status quo. The result was that conformist culture of the early 1950s gave way to the counterculture of the 1960s and the dramatic changes that followed. Rodman is a professor of communications at the University of South Florida and the author of *Elvis After Elvis: The Posthumous Career of a Living Legend*, from which the following is excerpted.

What I want to argue here is that [renowned composer and conductor Leonard] Bernstein's claim—that Elvis is "the greatest cultural force in the twentieth century"—is a legitimate one, not so much because of the music that Elvis made, but because of the previously unimagined realm of possibilities that Elvis's rise to prominence opened up for the ways that people could live and move through their daily lives.

Put in more theoretically sophisticated terms, my claim here is that Elvis was the point of articulation around which a new *cultural formation*—the one that crystallized around rock 'n' roll and ultimately went on to reshape mainstream US culture in dramatic and unprecedented ways—could come into existence. As [cultural studies researcher Larry] Grossberg describes it, a cultural formation is more than just a set of generically related texts; instead, it is defined by the ways in which

> a set of practices comes to congeal and, for a certain period of time, take on an identity of its own which is capable of existing in different social and cultural contexts. Unlike notions of genre, which assume that such identities depend on the existence of necessary formal elements, a formation is a historical articulation, an accumulation or organization of practices. . . .

ELVIS AS A CULTURAL FORCE RATHER THAN A MUSICIAN

To avoid misunderstanding, I should emphasize that there would unquestionably have been rock 'n' roll *music* without Elvis (though even here Elvis's importance often goes unacknowledged), if for no other reason than that a great deal of rock 'n' roll music had already been made prior to Elvis's arrival on the scene. It's not at all clear, however, that this musical genre would have given rise to a cultural formation (or at least not one of any prominence or lasting significance) had Elvis followed some life path other than the one that led him to rock 'n' roll (e.g., if he'd stuck with his career as a truck driver). One can of course point to countless other figures from the early days of rock 'n' roll (e.g., Chuck Berry, Bo Diddley, Fats Domino, Buddy Holly, Jerry Lee Lewis, Little Richard) who had more musical talent (at least as the term is typically understood) than Elvis ever had, and who were thus probably more important to defining the *sound* of rock 'n' roll than he was. Elvis, on the other hand, is a pivotal figure in rock 'n' roll history, not so much for what he contributed musically, but for what he contributed culturally. Put simply, no other musician had anything close to the combination of charisma, ambition, determination, talent, and instinctive media savvy that Elvis did; while other artists may have made greater music, no one else could have accomplished what Elvis did in terms of bringing together a vast range of musical genres, attitudes, styles of dress, behaviors, and other social practices in such a way that a coherent cultural formation could come into existence. Elvis changed the ways that people viewed the world in which they lived and, in doing so, he brought about significant changes in the ways that those people could—and did—live their lives. It was as if the old map of the cultural terrain had been torn up, the pieces burned, the ashes scattered to the four winds, and the whole thing replaced with a radically different diagram of that same territory—so different that it's easy to believe that this new map described an entirely new territory altogether. Which, after a fashion, it did, as this map opened up vast uncharted regions of possibility for how people could walk and talk and move through their daily lives; and, in doing so, it reshaped the hopes and aspirations of many of those people as to what sort of future they could (and would) build for themselves.

Admittedly, these are broad and sweeping claims to make on Elvis's behalf—so much so, in fact, that it's probably impossible to demonstrate their validity in a rigorous or conclusive fashion. In thinking about culture as a phenomenon in constant flux—one that only exists in the dialectical tensions between a society's "arts and learning" and its "whole way of life"—seemingly the only viable alternative to making overly broad macro-level generalizations is to collect and relate a vast range of individual anecdotes about the changes that took place in the daily lives of otherwise unconnected people. This methodological nightmare . . . is probably another reason for the widespread acceptance of a strictly textual model of culture: mapping out all (or even most) of the relevant facets of a cultural formation (e.g., describing the complex relationships that exist between a major public figure, his or her work, and the daily lives of the countless people affected by that work) in any detail is a monumental, if not impossible, task. It's much easier—albeit ultimately less accurate—to talk about culture in terms of texts, and to talk about cultural change in terms of the influence that one artist's or critic's texts have on that of other artists or critics.

How Elvis Changed Individual Lives

In the end, however, if those texts actually have a significant impact on the shape of the broader cultural terrain, it's *only* because they generate changes at the more local level of individual people and their daily lives first. Consequently, the place where we need to begin our attempt to comprehend the specific shape of the cultural formation that arose around rock 'n' roll is with the tales that people tell about how their lives were changed by what Elvis did in the mid-1950s. Typically, such testimonials are centered not on specific texts (e.g., " 'Don't Be Cruel' came on the radio for the first time and I thought it was the greatest record I'd ever heard") or on Elvis's impact on the broader US soundscape (e.g., "he changed the face of popular music forever"), but on a wider range of more personal—and ultimately more idiosyncratic—social practices: attitudes, dreams, hopes, aspirations, fashions, lifestyles, and so on.

Take, for instance, Sun Records stable-mate Carl Perkins' assessment of Elvis's impact, which doesn't mention music at all: "He never really died and never will. You don't change as much of the world as Elvis Presley changed—hair styles, clothes, moods, looks, sideburns—dad gum! He cut a path through this world! He's gonna be history, man. And he should be." Similarly, rock critic Tom Smucker recalls Elvis circa 1956 not as a great singer or a charismatic pop star, but as a disruptive force whose rise to prominence called the basic premises of (white, middle-class, suburban) daily life in the US in the 1950s into question at a very personal level. For Smucker, Elvis matters because he was "the man whose TV appearance inspires my brother to threaten to wear *blue jeans to church*.": at the heart of Smucker's story, we don't find Elvis's music; we find his public persona (his attitude, his style, his personality, etc.). Thus, in the end, the most significant changes that Elvis brought about are not textual in nature (e.g., the fact that Elvis's records begat and/or inspired subsequent great music) as much as they are social (e.g., the fact that Elvis could dramatically restructure the perspective that Smucker's brother had on the world in which he lived).

At one level, of course, Smucker's story is merely a trivial (if amusing) anecdote, as it seems safe to say that Elvis didn't inspire an entire generation of teenagers to rebel against the dress codes of their families' places of worship. What matters about this tale, however, isn't the particular incident in an individual's life that it describes as much as the broader shift in the attitudes and behaviors of a larger population that it represents. As Bruce Springsteen once described Elvis's impact, "It was like he came along and whispered a dream in everybody's ear and then we dreamed it." One of the reasons why it's so difficult to recognize (much less describe) the extent to which Elvis reshaped US culture, however, is that the specific ways that different people tried to live out the dream that Springsteen mentions varied dramatically from person to person, and these attempts usually didn't take place in highly visible corners of the public sphere. For Smucker's brother, that dream manifested itself in a relatively private act of sartorial rebellion against his parents and their church: a transgression that presumably led to similar acts of rebellion (perhaps on a larger scale) later on in life. For Springsteen, that dream revolved around trying to do with his own life what Elvis was doing: "I remember when I was nine years old," Springsteen told the crowd at a 1981 concert, "and I was sittin' in front of the TV set and my mother had Ed Sullivan on and on came Elvis. I remember right from that time, I looked at her and said, 'I wanna be *just . . . like . . . that.*'" For millions of others, that dream undoubtedly took millions of other shapes, no two of which were quite the same and very few of which ever attracted widespread public attention (e.g., it was nearly twenty years before Springsteen's attempt to live out that dream became obvious to the general public and, even then, his success in living out that dream is undoubtedly an exception to the rule).

ELVIS'S VERSION OF THE AMERICAN DREAM

In many respects, this dream was more or less a revamped version of the American Dream: it still involved a fairly idealistic (and perhaps even naïve) vision of equal opportunity and upward mobility (e.g., anyone can become a star), and its ultimate goal was still firmly tied to the economic rewards of "making it big." What was different about Elvis's version of the Dream, however, was the path to its achievement: eschewing the classic Puritan ethic, where hard work was the necessary (albeit unglamorous) route to the proverbial top, the dream that Elvis whispered in a nation's collective ear was that one could have it all *while* or *by* (rather than *instead of*) having fun. [Rock critic Greil Marcus writes:]

> the idea (and it was just barely an "idea") that Saturday night [i.e., the brief and transient moments of hedonistic pleasure that are the secondary reward for a never-ending routine of hard work] could be the whole show. You had to be young and a bit insulated to pull it off, but why not? Why not trade pain and boredom for kicks and style? Why not make an escape from a way of life . . . into a way of life?

The idea itself isn't entirely new—Elvis undoubtedly picked it up from the comic books and Hollywood movies that he consumed so assiduously as a child, and Marcus points out that Twain closes *Huckleberry Finn* on much the same note—but prior to Elvis that was all it was: a fantasy that worked well on the silver screen and in the pages of novels, but not an idea that one could reasonably expect would ever come to fruition in the real world—not until Elvis came along, that is, and demonstrated otherwise. . . .

. . . Or at least he *seemed* to do so. The skeptical reader will no doubt claim that Elvis ultimately served as a very poor example of this dream in action. Fans and critics will probably argue forever about just when Elvis's story began to turn sour on him (was it when he first hooked up with Colonel Parker? the day his draft notice arrived? when he sold his soul to Hollywood and/or Vegas? etc.), but they almost all agree that, at some point, Elvis's dream collapsed back in upon itself and smothered him. The Elvis who died, bloated, full of pills, and on the toilet, was a nightmarish parody of the brash and exciting young upstart who remade US culture with a thrust of his hips twenty years earlier, and thus the moral behind Elvis's story is a reaffirmation of what we'd already known: that dreams such as his only come true in fairy tales and movies. Even Springsteen concludes his anecdote about seeing Elvis on television in the 1950s by saying:

> But then I grew up and I didn't want to be just like that [i.e., like Elvis] no more. . . . I thought a lot about it—how somebody who could've had so much could in the end lose so bad and how dreams don't mean nothin' unless you're strong enough to fight for 'em and make 'em come true. You gotta hold onto yourself. [Quoted in music critic Dave Marsh's book *Glory Days*.]

What Marsh doesn't tell us about this particular moment from Springsteen's 1981 tour is what song he introduced with this story. It's not unreasonable to think that it might have been "Johnny Bye Bye" (a Springsteen B-side from 1985 that describes Elvis's undignified demise in poignant, but unromanticized, terms), or maybe even "Follow That Dream" (a 1962 Elvis hit that Springsteen has been known to perform in concert). The ending that I imagine to this story, however, has Springsteen going on to perform "The River" (1980), which is *not* about Elvis, but it *is* about the disparity between the dreams that people have for their lives and the less than dreamlike ways that those lives often turn out: "Is a dream a lie if it don't come true?" Springsteen asks at the end of the song's final verse, "Or is it something worse?" This, after all, is the question that many people asked—and are still asking—in the wake of Elvis's surprising and undignified death: an event that (coupled with the host of post-mortem revelations concerning Elvis's descent into paranoia, violent outbursts, and prescription drug abuse) called into question the value (and the validity) of the dream that he'd represented to so many people for so long.

TRANSFORMING A GENERATION

But no matter how disillusioning the nature of his decline was, the fact remains that Elvis's primary impact on US culture needs to be measured, not by how his story ended, but by how it began . . . and, in the beginning, Elvis successfully convinced a generation that they didn't have to dream the same dreams—which is to say that they didn't have to live the same lives—that their parents had settled for. Despite the fact that the dream he whispered in a nation's ear was ultimately an unattainable one for most people (i.e., not everyone could become a star of Elvis's—or even Springsteen's—magnitude), the actual process of millions of people trying to follow that dream and make it a reality was enough to transform US culture in untold ways. As Marcus puts it,

> rock 'n' roll caught that romantic conspiracy ["a cosmic conspiracy against reality in favor of romance"] on records and gave it a form. Instead of a possibility within a music, it became the essence; it became, of all things, a tradition. And when that form itself had to deal with reality—which is to say, when its young audience began to grow up— . . . the fantasy had become part of the reality that had to be dealt with; the rules of the game had changed a bit, and it was a better game.

Marcus's last sentence contains an implicit acknowledgment that, at one level, rock 'n' roll fell short of whatever revolutionary goals it purported to have for itself: that its attempt "to make an escape from a way of life . . . into a way of life" didn't actually dismantle the central structures and institutions of the old culture as much as it pretended (or tried to) that those institutions could simply be ignored or dismissed out of hand. At the same time, however, Marcus's comments point out that the failure of that revolution (i.e., the fact that rock 'n' roll ultimately found itself allied with, and even at the center of, the mainstream culture to which it had supposedly stood in opposition) was only a partial one, insofar as rock 'n' roll *did* manage to alter the shape of mainstream US culture in significant ways: that, despite the fact that the revolutionary threat of rock 'n' roll was quietly nullified and reabsorbed into the mainstream culture, the world was still a more exciting and interesting place *with* rock 'n' roll in it than it could ever have been without it.

ELVIS LAID THE FOUNDATIONS OF 1960s COUNTERCULTURE

In the end, the "better game" to which Marcus alludes played itself out in a number of different ways, as the dream that Elvis gave the country took a wide range of idiosyncratic and personalized forms. And when those dreams met up with one another on the broader terrain of US culture, they added up to more than the sum of their individual parts; they called a new "community" into existence, a community defined by and centered around the budding cultural formation associated with rock 'n' roll. [*LA Weekly* columnist Michael Ventura writes:]

> When Elvis Presley hit the charts in 1956 there was no such thing as a "youth market." By 1957, almost solely through the demand for his recordings, there was. It was a fundamental, structural change in American society. In a few years we would learn *how* fundamental, as that "market" revealed itself also to have qualities of a community, one that had the power to initiate far-reaching social changes that seemed unimaginable in 1955. The antiwar movement, the second wave of the civil-rights movement, feminism, ecology, and the higher consciousness movement . . . got their impetus from the excitement of people who felt strong because they felt they were part of a national community of youth, a community that had first been defined, and then often inspired, by its affinity for this music. *That* was the public, historical result of those private epiphanies of personal energy we'd felt through this music's form of possession.

In essence, Ventura is crediting Elvis with triggering most (if not all) of the social and cultural upheavals that would come into their own in the 1960s—and he's far from alone in making such a claim: [rock critic] Lester Bangs, Leonard Bernstein, and [poet and musician] John Trudell (among others) have also argued that Elvis was responsible for the various cultural transformations that took place in the US in the decade after he first burst into national prominence.

Now, at first glance, such an argument seems even more untenable than the notion that a reasonable person could use the words "Elvis" and "culture" in the same sentence with a straight face. Elvis, after all, deliberately shied away from mixing music and politics—or even from expressing his political convictions in public—and he was far too "straight" to be plausibly seen as a hippie sympathizer (much less as an actual hippie himself). What Ventura *et al.* are claiming, however, is not that Elvis somehow embodied "the Sixties," but that, culturally speaking, he laid the foundation that made "the Sixties" possible in the first place: that, without Elvis, contemporary US culture would look and feel remarkably like the pre-Elvis culture of the early 1950s. Novelist and short story writer Chet Williamson describes such a world this way:

> Everybody on the street looked like their parents. There were square clothes, butch-waxed haircuts, horn-rimmed glasses, and big round cars, like whales in pastel shades, driving down the streets. The gay bookstore [i.e., the one that exists in "our" Elvis-filled world] was a Christian Science Reading Room, and the Hard Rock [Cafe] was, God help me, a Howard Johnson's restaurant and "cocktail lounge." . . . Rock and roll was an underground music, tolerated by society and centered in "Negro" (as they were still called) communities. *All the changes that had come about in the sixties never occurred.* We were still in Nam, civil rights was nothing but a dream for blacks, gays still hid their inclinations, and the Cold War was iced over so hard it would never thaw out. People didn't know how to rebel. And the only conclusion that I can draw is that *it was because they never had an Elvis Presley to teach them, to show them how to sneer, and how to assault their elders with music.* (emphasis added)

Like Smucker, Williamson is arguing for Elvis's importance not on musical grounds as much as he is on social and attitudinal ones: the world that Williamson describes still has rock 'n' roll *music,* but the *cultural formation* centered around that music—if it exists at all—is marginalized in what are presumably separate-but-not-all-that-equal "Negro communities." Elvis changed the world not by introducing (or even popularizing) rock 'n' roll as a musical sound, but by teaching audiences in the 1950s how to question—and, at times, rebel against—authority.

DISCUSSION QUESTIONS

CHAPTER ONE

1. Describe Elvis's parents and his relationship with them, particularly the ways in which Gladys Presley encouraged Elvis as a child.

2. John Shelton Reed describes the town of Tupelo, Mississippi, as it was during Elvis's boyhood. What aspects of life in Tupelo do you think may have most affected the young Elvis?

3. Rupert Matthews describes how Colonel Tom Parker first helped Elvis "hit the big time." What examples does the author provide of how the Colonel may have negatively impacted Elvis's career? Can you provide examples from other readings in which the Colonel is depicted as selfish or greedy?

CHAPTER TWO

1. Elvis's rise to fame occurred quickly: Only twenty-five months elapsed between the release of his first record and his famous appearance on *The Ed Sullivan Show*. List the key events that led to the "Elvis mania" David P. Szatmary describes in his essay.

2. What three trends in the 1950s does Patsy Guy Hammontree say paved the way for a "musical watershed"?

CHAPTER THREE

1. Linda Martin and Kerry Segrave quote many of the criticisms and attacks directed at Elvis just after he became popular in 1954. Can you sympathize with the parents and community leaders of the 1950s who feared that Elvis was a bad influence on the nation's youth, or do you feel the backlash directed at Elvis was unwarranted or excessive? Explain your answer.

2. According to Peter Wicke, what aspects of life in the 1950s made teenagers restless and ready to latch onto a new musical trend? In his opinion, what was it about Elvis that made him so fascinating to teenagers of the era?

3. Leonard Pitts Jr. states that he originally thought of Elvis as "an interloper who raided black culture and exploited it," but has since come to think of Elvis as a person who "brought separations together" and "revealed segregation as a lie." Do you agree that Elvis had a positive effect on race relations, or do you think Pitts's original view, that Elvis's success was based on cultural theft, has merit?

CHAPTER FOUR

1. Contrast Jerry Hopkins's depiction of Elvis's comeback performance in Las Vegas with Roy Carr and Mick Farren's description of Elvis's *Aloha from Hawaii* television special. Are these authors being completely objective in their portrayals, or their own personal views of Elvis apparent in their essays? Explain.

2. Do you feel that the unsavory circumstances of Elvis's final years, including his drug addiction and bizarre behavior, detract from his earlier successes? Why or why not?

CHAPTER FIVE

1. Decades after his death, the public's fascination with Elvis is alive and well. List some of the various ways that Elvis fans keep his memory alive.

2. James Miller writes that for many rock and roll audiences, the music has taken on a religious aspect. He notes that Elvis was only the first of many rock stars to be idolized by fans after an early death. Can you name other modern performers who have developed the cultlike following the author describes?

3. Gilbert B. Rodman argues that "Elvis changed the ways that people viewed the world in which they lived." What does he mean by this, and what evidence does he use to support this belief?

APPENDIX OF DOCUMENTS

DOCUMENT 1: HILLBILLY ON A PEDESTAL

In May of 1956 Newsweek *became one of the first national periodicals to report on Elvis's rapid rise to fame. In an article titled "Hillbilly on a Pedestal," the news magazine profiles Elvis and describes rock and roll as "a new kind of music, in general vogue."*

The high-pitched squeals of females in fanatic teen-age packs are being heard again. Elvis Presley, a hillbilly singer capable of impressive bodily contortions, has moved onto the pedestal lately occupied by Johnnie Ray and, before him, by Frank Sinatra.

Girls describe Presley as a combination of Marlon Brando and the late James Dean, and boys admire the exaggeration of his rhythmic rock 'n' roll. (Alleged to be a new kind of music, in general vogue since the song "Rock Around the Clock" was used in "Blackboard Jungle" in 1954, rock 'n' roll is actually a coarsened version of what a "jump" band like Count Basie's does with refinement.)

Presley's latest record hit, on RCA Victor, "Heartbreak Hotel," has passed the million mark: his album, "Elvis Presley," has sold more than 362,000 copies since its release in mid-March, an RCA Victor record in quick sales.

"SO MEAN"

The impact of Presley in personal appearances has so far been felt only in the Southeast and Southwest. Presley's tour in Texas last month produced delirious mob scenes in San Antonio. Typical female comments: "I like him because he looks so mean"; "He's fascinating—like a snake"; "I hear he peddles dope"; "He's been in and out of jail, and he's gonna die of cancer in six months." A local reviewer (adult and male) was less impressed: "Presley is more of a male burlesque queen than anything else."

Last week Presley wound up his first night-club date, a two-week stand at the New Frontier Hotel in Las Vegas. Wedged into a show built around Freddy Martin's silken arrangements of Tchaikowsky and show tunes, Elvis was somewhat like a jug of corn liquor at a champagne party. He hollered songs like "Blue Suede Shoes" and "Heartbreak Hotel," and his bodily motions were embarrassingly specific. Most of the slick, moneyed audience sighed with relief when Martin took over again, having sat through Presley as if he were a clinical experiment. Elvis's comment: "I don't want no more night clubs. An audience like this don't show their appreciation the same way. They're eating when I come on."

PINK CAD

At 21, Elvis has three Cadillacs, one Messerschmitt tricycle car, and a house for his parents in Memphis, where he went to live after his boyhood in Tupelo, Miss. He does not drink or smoke. "I used to be on a pink-and-black kick," he says. "Pink-and-black shirts, even a pink-and-black Cad. I got sick of it." He also likes to shoot pool and visit penny arcades. "I won 24 Teddy bears at a fair once. People was giving me money to win them one."

Presley has been given a standard seven-year contract with Hal Wallis–Paramount. "I wouldn't want no regular spot on no TV program," he says. "Movies are the thing. I love to act. I don't care nothing whatsoever about singing in no movie. English was what I liked best in high school. I want to be a dramatic actor. Some day I want to write a book. About what it's like to be an entertainer. It's tough, man, tough."

Reprinted from "Hillbilly on a Pedestal," *Newsweek*, May 14, 1956. Copyright © 1956 by Newsweek, Inc. Reprinted with permission. All rights reserved.

DOCUMENT 2: A THREAT TO THE NATION'S YOUTH

From the start, Elvis's concerts were controversial, as parents worried about the hysteria Elvis inspired in his teenage fans. The following document is a letter written by a concerned adult to former FBI director J. Edgar Hoover, dated May 16, 1956. Based on the chaos surrounding an Elvis concert in La Crosse, Wisconsin, the letter-writer (whose name has been sealed by the FBI) warns that Elvis may be "both a drug addict and a sexual pervert" and a "definite danger to the security of the United States."

The letter became part of the FBI's growing file on Presley, portions of which are now available to the public under the Freedom of Information Act at http://foia.fbi.gov/presley.htm.

Dear Mr. Hoover,

Elvis Presley, press-agented as a singer and entertainer, played to two groups of teenagers numbering several thousand at the city auditorium here, Monday, May 14.

As newspaper man, parent, and former member of Army Intelligence Service, I feel an obligation to pass on to you my conviction that Presley is a definite danger to the security of the United States.

Although I could not attend myself, I sent two reporters to cover his second show at 9:30 P.M. Besides, I secured the opinions of others of good judgment, who had seen the show or had heard direct reports of it. Among them are a radio station manager, a former motion picture exhibitor, an orchestra player, and a young woman employee of a radio station who witnessed the show to determine its value. All agree that it was the filthiest and most harmful production that ever came to La Crosse for exhibition to teenagers.

When Presley came on the stage, the youngsters almost mobbed him. . . . The audience could not hear his "singing" for the screaming and carrying on of the teenagers.

But eye-witnesses have told me that Presley's actions and motions were such as to rouse the sexual passions of teenaged youth.

One eye-witness described his actions as "sexual self-gratification on the stage,"—another as "a strip-tease with clothes on." Although police and auxiliaries were there, the show went on. Perhaps the hardened police did not get the import of his motions and gestures, like those of masturbation or riding a microphone. (The assistant district attorney and Captain William Boma also stopped in for a few minutes in response to complaints about the first show, but they found no reason to halt the show.)

After the show, more than 1,000 teenagers tried to gang into Presley's room at the auditorium, then at the Stoddard Hotel. All possible police on duty were necessary at the Hotel to keep watch on the teenagers milling about the hotel till after 3 A.M., the hotel manager informed me. Some kept milling about the city till about 5 A.M.

Indications of the harm Presley did just in La Crosse were the two high school girls (of whom I have direct personal knowledge) whose abdomen and thigh had Presley's autograph. They admitted that they went to his room where this happened. It is known by psychologists, psychiatrists and priests that teenaged girls from the age of eleven, and boys in their adolescence, are easily aroused to sexual indulgence and perversion by certain types of motions and hysteria,—the type that was exhibited at the Presley show.

There is also gossip of the Presley Fan Clubs that degenerate into sex orgies. The local radio station WKBH sponsors a club on the "Lindy Shannon Show."

From eye-witness reports about Presley, I would judge that he may possibly be both a drug addict and a sexual pervert. In any case I am sure he bears close watch,—especially in the face of growing juvenile crime nearly everywhere in the United States. He is surrounded by a group of high-pressure agents who seem to control him, the hotel manager reported.

I do not report idly to the FBI. My last official report to an FBI agent in New York before I entered the U.S. Army resulted in arrest of a saboteur (who committed suicide before his trial). I believe the Presley matter is as serious to U.S. security. I am convinced that juvenile crimes of lust and perversion will follow his show here in La Crosse. . . .

Only a moron could not see the connection between the Presley exhibit and the incidence of teenage disorders in La Crosse.

Letter to J. Edgar Hoover, May 16, 1956. Available at http://foia.fbi.gov/presley.htm.

DOCUMENT 5: THE DEBUT OF *LOVE ME TENDER*

In the following review of Elvis's first movie, Love Me Tender, which debuted in November 1956, critic Gerald Weales laments that film heroes such as the one Elvis portrays increasingly behave more like adolescents than adults.

They are all gone or going, the film heroes of my youth—the strong, silent type, the fast-talking wiseacre, the sophisticated man of the world. All are going to pasture to make way for the movie hero of the 1950's, and he seems to be a cross between Peck's Bad Boy and Rebecca of Sunnybrook Farm.

In his latest, most grotesque form the new hero is Elvis Presley, who has climbed out of the nation's juke boxes onto its screens in a limp, lusterless Western, "Love Me Tender." Judging by the absence of crowds outside the Paramount Theater, where the film is making its New York debut, and by the restraint of the audience inside (only an occasional squeal), "Love Me Tender" is not likely to add anyone to Presley's profitable following, for his best-selling records have already given him the kind of celebrity that inspired excited fans to rip his clothes off in a Midwestern appearance last summer. His role in the film—that of a young man who looks up longingly and then jealously at his older brother—is particularly tailored to his appearance, for Presley resembles an obscene child, a too sensuous adolescent. He cannot hope to reach his brother's manliness, so he conveniently gets killed and then appears, a memory in the sky, like Jeanette MacDonald in "Smilin' Through," intoning the title song while the rest of the characters move drably across the hillside.

The film's function, of course, is not to provide a role at all, but simply an excuse for four Presley songs. His voice with its characteristic quaver, its vacillation between a shout and a whine, is the culmination of all the song criers who have been popular since the Second World War. In performance, he uses his guitar as a fetish, pounding his pelvis against it, a strident symbol that here is another of those tough, sensitive kids, one of the little boys who know what the big boys do.

Presley, however, is not to blame for the dethronement of the adult film hero, for he is simply a variant in a long line of adolescent leads. No one is to blame, I suppose. Not Marlon Brando, who first gave the new hero film form and made him popular. Not Jimmy Dean, who became the center of a posthumous cult. Not Lee Strasberg, whose Actors' Studio is supposed to be the home of the new hero's acting style. Not even the kids in blue jeans and leather jackets, both boys and girls, who carry the pictures of Brando and Dean, of Elvis and Sal Mineo in their wallets. It's just that the apotheosis of the immature has finally hit Hollywood.

Who is the new hero? How does he look, move, talk, and dress? . . .

First of all, he does not walk: he slouches, ambles, almost minces. His hand gestures are all tentative, incomplete, with arms out in front as though he were feeling his way along a wet-walled underground passageway, or folded back against the body as though he were warding off a blow. Although he is a tough guy, his face is excessively sensitive, almost effeminate, with full-lipped pout and large-eyed lostness.

His dress is the uniform of his admirers—the jeans, the sweatshirt, the leather jacket—but even in suit and tie he looks casual and undressed. He speaks in jagged, broken bits of sentences, disconnected words, sudden cries of pain and incoherence; inarticulateness is his trademark.

The new hero is an adolescent. Whether he is twenty or thirty or forty, he is fifteen and excessively sorry for himself. He is essentially a lone wolf who wants to belong, but even when he is the member of a gang or a group he is still alone. He is the victim of parents who do not understand him and whom he does not understand. Sometimes they love him too much, sometimes not at all: sometimes he hates them, sometimes he idolizes them. In the long run it is all one; he is loveless and wants to be loving. Since he is inarticulate, he cannot cry out his hunger: he can only communicate through a random kind of violence, which the films can best express by using motorcycles and hot rods.

Gerald Weales, "Movies: The Crazy, Mixed-Up Kids Take Over," *Reporter*, December 13, 1956.

DOCUMENT 4: ELVIS, TEEN IDOL

By 1957, most of the initial concerns that Elvis might pose a "threat" to the nation's youth had died down. But many critics remained convinced that rock and roll was having a coarsening effect on American culture and that teenagers' obsession with Elvis led them to ignore classical music. The following document is a newspaper article in which columnist George E. Sokolsky criticizes Elvis and rock and roll in general. Sokolsky was responding to a letter from a teenage Elvis fan, who was in turn writing to protest an earlier column by Sokolsky in which he claimed that Elvis's popularity was a passing fad.

I received a most instructive letter from Miss Charlotte Jones of Dallas, Texas, which I am herewith reproducing in full as a contribution to Americana. Here is the letter:

"Dear Mr. Sokolsky:
"There are too many people saying that Elvis is going to die out. When Elvis dies out is when the sun quits burnin.
"You say everybody is forgotten that is once great: George Washington has never been forgotten and nobody can ever be as great a president or as long remembered as he. Nobody can ever take his place or do what he did. Well, it's the same with Elvis. He'll always be remembered and nobody has ever or ever will do the same thing as Elvis has. Elvis is the king of popularity and we (teens of America) love him and we'll see he lives forever. Not his body but his name. Adults won't admit he's so great, because they're jealous! They know that their top singers weren't as great as Elvis. They're mad because their taste isn't quite as good as ours.
"Look at James Dean, been dead for a year and he's bigger now than he ever was.
"God gifted Elvis to us and you oughta thank him, not tear down, the greatest thing the world ever known: Elvis Presley!!!!!!
                                    Scornfully yours,
                                    Charlotte Jones
"P. S.: And if you're over 30, you're old. You're certainly not young."

It shows the advantage of an education, that Miss Jones compares Elvis Presley's accomplishments with those of George Washington. Of course, as history goes, Washington has not been so long remembered; he only died in 1799 which is not long ago compared with Alexander the Great, or Julius Caesar or, on the peaceful side, with Hammurabi, Moses or Solon. Nevertheless, it must be admitted that Miss Jones has a point and that George Washington is today better remembered than many another president and plenty of kings.

I find it hard quite to realize what is meant by "the king of popularity." Does Miss Jones really believe that Elvis is more popular than President Eisenhower or General Douglas MacArthur or the Queen of England or Dr. Albert Schweitzer? If that is so, then why should men devote themselves to noble deeds and great accomplishments? Why not just warble an old Civil War song and twang a banjo and achieve the accolade that way?

Apparently all adults are jealous of this Elvis, otherwise they would acknowledge that his voice is superior to Caruso's; his profile to John Barrymore's; his acting to E.H. Sothern's. Miss Jones's knowledge must be like Teddy Nadler's who said something the other day about having a tremendous knowledge of classical music. But what has he done with that knowledge? That is always the question.

She Likes What She Likes

I have no idea how old Charlotte Jones is. She does not introduce herself with vital statistics. But she does believe that she and her "teens" have better taste than her elders, by which she means that she likes what she likes and that anyone who disagrees is a square, a jerk or a dope. Could be.

Yet, I wonder what would happen to such a hero worshipper if she spent six weeks next summer at Tanglewood listening to Bach, Mozart, Beethoven, Brahms and Tschaikovsky. All long-hair, it is true. But music is music and is supposed to thrill the heart of civilized and savage. It would be an interesting experiment, like bringing Tarzan to the Colony Restaurant or Pavilion, to eat food as designed by Escoffier.

The real point of this letter is that it displays no cultural background. I heard Elvis sing and I believe that perhaps in five years or so, he might be able to carry a tune as well as Bing Crosby. But in 50 years, he could not make the chorus of the Metropolitan Opera.

The fault undoubtedly is in a school system which gives the child so little cultural background, so little basis for taste and so little understanding of beauty. Rock-N-Roll, which is a musical reversion to the tom-tom of the jungle, can stir so many of our young to ecstasy only because they know no better. It is curious that in a Western country a child could write, "The greatest thing the world has ever known: Elvis Presley." I used to hear them say that that title went to Jesus. How times do change!

Reprinted from "She Believes Elvis Is 'The Greatest,'" by George E. Sokolsky, *New York Journal-American*, March 11, 1957.

DOCUMENT 5: EXPLAINING THE ELVIS PHENOMENON

By 1958, critics were already beginning to examine the enormous in-fluence that Elvis had had on U.S. culture in his two years of fame. In the following article, James and Annette Baxter attempt to ex-plain Elvis's appeal to teenagers and conclude that Elvis's influence on youth is not as bad as many people had claimed.

As a subject for polemic Elvis Presley has few peers, and too many people have experienced sudden shifts in blood pressure—either up or down—for him to be regarded as anything but an authentic barometer of the times. But, even now that he has been on the na-tional scene for more than two years, he may be telling us more about ourselves than we would care to admit.

Presley's climb to fame, in the winter of 1955–56, followed upon the appearance of that raucous brand of popular music, primitive and heavy-footed, known as rock-and-roll. Untouched by subtlety, rock-and-roll seemed to signal a total collapse in popular taste, the final schism between a diminishing group sensitive to tradition and the great bulk of those who make entertainment to sell. Sud-denly there was Elvis, not merely a manifestation of rock-and-roll, but of lascivious gyrations of the torso that older generations quickly recognized—the classic bump and grind of the strip-teaser.

"THE PELVIS"

Television compounded the jeopardy: Elvis could come lurching into any living-room, and he did, and the chorus of adolescent shrieks was swelled by shrieks from the parents. The stomping bla-tancy of "Blue Suede Shoes" and the insinuations of "I Want You, I Need You, I Love You" were sufficiently distressing, but the foot-spread stance and the unmistakable thrust—well, "The Pelvis" was going too far. . . .

Admonished that there were those who found his hip-swiveling offensive, Elvis is said to have replied, "I never made no dirty body movements." And this is believable; Elvis moves as the spirit moves him; it all comes naturally. Hormones flow in him as serenely as the Mississippi past Memphis, and the offense lies in the eye of the beholder, not in Elvis' intentions.

By constantly reminding his teen-age listeners of what he so ob-viously was—a simple boy from Tupelo who had suddenly become famous—Elvis somehow removed the sting from the sexuality that could easily have terrified them. Valentino had to become an exotic in order to keep from frightening the ladies of an earlier era with his own heavy-lidded gaze: Elvis could remain the boy next door. He was even able to capitalize on his innocence: in his television appearances he could find himself flinging a Svengali-like finger out toward his audience and, when they squealed, he couldn't keep from giggling. He was as amused as they were by his idiotic power to hypnotize and, although the spell was on, the curse was off.

But Presley's stunning rapport with his own generation must hinge on something more than the ageless call of the wild. Appealing to the youthful imagination in some way inscrutable to the parents of the teen-agers who worship him, Elvis fills some kind of need that the older generation can't fathom, and more significantly, doesn't feel. Why? Perhaps because they have run out of dreams.

Parents for whom the introduction of television in the late 'forties begat the era of the great giveaway need no dreams—they are already living one. Ranch-style homes, organization-man jobs, and exalted community status have outrun whatever hopes they brought from a meager past, and adults are too delightedly clutching these tangible evidences of a dream-come-true to bother projecting a more fanciful one. Their smartly-executed station-wagon psyches, jauntily upholstered and gleamingly trimmed, leave no room for excrescences and irrelevancies. But their offspring, a generation of poor little rich children, whom no part of the postwar bonanza has the power to enthrall, remain desperately in need of an enchanter.

THE MYSTERIOUS SOUTH

To meet this historic contingency Elvis is blessed not only with sex but with authentic Southernness. His primitivism carries conviction; when he intones the monotonous phrases of "I Got a Woman," Southern medium espouses Southern temperament. . . .

The sum of Presley's qualities matches the national image of the Southland. For the South today popularly represents what the West once did: the self-sufficient, the inaccessible, the fiercely independent soul of the nation. With the taming of the West completed, only the deep South retains a comparable aura of mystery, of romantic removal from the concerns of a steadily urbanized and cosmopolized America. . . .

The adolescent is far more responsive to [Elvis] than his parents could be. In the backwoods heterodoxies of Elvis he recognizes a counterpart to his own instinctive rebellion. And when Elvis confesses that he's "Gonna Sit Right Down and Cry," the accents of lament are felt as genuine; there's none of the artifice of the torch-singer in his wail. Elvis is for real, and in his voice the teen-ager hears intimations of a world heavily weighted with real emotion. . . .

Ultimately the music Elvis makes must be given some credit for his popularity. And there is probably an ugly, awesome little truth in the deduction that he is prodigiously gifted. To those attentive to the music itself the most conspicuous feature of Elvis' singing is the versatility with which he exploits the tradition of the Negro "blues-shouter." He can shift without apparent strain from the blasting stridency of "Hound Dog" to the saccharine ooze of "I'll Never Let You Go," covering, when called upon, every transitional pose between: the choke-and-groan of "Love Me," the plaintive nasal whine of "How's the World Treating You," the gravel-throated bellow of "Long Tall Sally," or the throb-and-tremolo of "I Got a Woman."

Vocal pyrotechnics he has indeed (to what must be the everlasting despair of his imitators), but they would remain merely curiosities were he not able to manipulate them into an organic whole. His twisting of a tonal quality possesses a diabolical inevitability, and his phrasing is as flawless as it is intricate. Marianne Moore's comment about e.e. cummings—"He does not make aesthetic mistakes"—might with only brief hesitation be applied to Elvis Presley. Elvis has got the beat, and "Don't Be Cruel" will bear scrutiny by any but the most outraged of his captious audience. . . .

A MORE RESPONSIBLE ELVIS?

Whither Presley? When his present public finds itself, as it someday must, demesmerized by time, and when the mage-like fascination of Elvis gives way to some new and less inspired teen-age melodrama, what's to become of this young man whose life and legend are by now indistinguishable?

Will Elvis himself be able to salvage a personality from among the accumulated debris of prolonged public exposure? Will he choose one of several paths systematically trodden by the once great: lucratively "advising" the producers of "The Elvis Presley Story," lecturing across the country on the prevention of juvenile delinquency, opening with moderate hoopla a restaurant in Atlantic City, appointing a respectable hack to ghost his memoirs, or posing rakishly for a Chesterfield ad?

Some indication that Elvis has a notion of the responsibility of his mission is his plan for a fifteen-acre Elvis Presley Youth Foundation in Tupelo, reported in *Time*. How far this project may go is uncertain, but if it takes him back to Mississippi for spiritual recuperation from time to time, it will be both good for him and for the youth who want him, need him, and love him.

Excerpted from "The Man in the Blue Suede Shoes," by James and Annette Baxter, *Harper's Magazine*, January 1958. Copyright © 1958 by Harper's Magazine. Reprinted from the January 1958 issue by special permission.

DOCUMENT 6: DRAFTED

Elvis's induction into the U.S. Army merited a short article in The New York Times.

America's rock 'n' roll idol held up his right hand today and took the oath that made him Pvt. Presley, Elvis A., Serial No. U.S. 53310761.

Mr. Presley, who is 23 years old, will have eight weeks of basic infantry training at Fort Chaffee, Ark. He and twenty other new soldiers left in a chartered bus. Mr. Presley was appointed "private in charge."

The nation's most celebrated draftee, whose voice has sold more than 22,000,000 records in less than three years, turned up half an hour early to begin his Army career.

The draft term is for two years. The salary cut is tremendous. As a private, Mr. Presley will draw $73 a month. Last year his gross income was nearly $1,000,000.

"It's only right that the draft applies to everybody alike," shrugged Mr. Presley. "Rich or poor, there should be no exceptions."

Reprinted from "King of Rock 'n' Roll Becomes Pvt. Presley," *The New York Times*, March 25, 1958.

DOCUMENT 7: BACK FROM GERMANY

On March 14, 1960, Life *magazine reported on Elvis's return from his army post in Germany, describing how Elvis's manager had helped maintain the singer's popularity during his two-year absence.*

In a spectacular shift of power that critically exposed the flank of U.S. music lovers, the Army returned US53310761 from Germany last week for mustering out at Fort Dix, N.J. Fans mobilized to fighting strength and tuned up their shrieks. Mimeographed directives sped from the Pentagon as the Army proudly staged a press conference. Elvis was back.

After his two-year hitch, 25-year-old rock 'n' roll idol Elvis Presley wore a sergeant's chevrons but no sideburns. "If I say the Army made a man of me," he said, "it would give the impression I was an idiot before I was drafted. I wasn't exactly that."

Elvis was, in fact, a smart soldier. His agents back home had been pretty smart too, selling 20 million RCA Victor records to the jukebox set. These earned "The Pelvis" $1.3 million in addition to his $145.24 a month service pay. Elvis paid the U.S. 91% of the total in taxes, or enough to support about 150 of his fellow soldiers for a year.

Behind him at Ray Barracks near Friedberg, Elvis had left hordes of palpitating *Fräuleins* and the pretty 16-year-old Priscilla Beaulieu, daughter of an Air Force captain stationed at Wiesbaden. Elvis kissed her before he flew to the aid of the girls back home, sorrowful at parting but anxious to get into his bright-colored pants and back to his hip-swinging singing.

Reprinted from "Sergeant Elvis Comes Back Home to the Girls He Left Behind Him," *Life*, March 14, 1960. Copyright © 1960 by Time, Inc. Reprinted with permission.

DOCUMENT 8: A TAMER ELVIS

Just weeks after Elvis returned from his stint in the army, a May 30, 1960, Newsweek *article asked, "Is This a 'New' Presley?" Already fans and the media were noticing that Elvis was downplaying his image as a rebel and spending more time acting in movies than he was making music.*

In his first movie after two Army years in Germany, ex-Sergeant Presley was playing, of all things, a soldier stationed in, of all places, Germany. The sideburns and 15 pounds of flesh were gone, but otherwise it was just like the old days—oceans of hubbub washing over the star who, as long as he wasn't singing, remained quiet, deferential, and serious. . . .

"If you don't mind, sir, I'll just keep my hat on while I eat," Elvis said, glancing at the air conditioner in his dressing room. "I got to keep this hair in place and I might catch a chill after that shower."

He began munching an unbuttered roll ("A lunch makes me sleepy") as he was asked about his Army stint. "I learned a lot about people in the Army," he said. "There was all different types. I never lived with other people before and had a chance to find out how they think. It sure changed me, but I can't tell you offhand just how. . . .

"I never griped. If I didn't like something, nobody knew, excepting me. Nothing bad happened. If I'd 'a' been what they thought, I'd have got what was coming to me. But I never talked about show business. I went along."

He was asked about his future plans.

"I'm ambitious to become a more serious actor, but I don't want to give up the music business by no means," he said. "I can't change my style, either. If I feel like moving around, I still move. As for the fans, they've changed some but they're still there, the same ones."

DOCUMENT 9: THE LAS VEGAS COMEBACK

In the following review of Elvis's first "comeback" performance in Las Vegas in 1969, New Yorker *critic Ellen Willis commends Elvis's more "mature" performance.*

When I heard that Presley had accepted an engagement at the new International Hotel in Las Vegas and was to give his first concert in nine years, I knew the confrontation had to be interesting. Elvis was at once old money and young money, sellout and folk hero. How would he play it? In his television special last winter, he wore a leather jacket and wiggled his hips. But then he recorded "In the Ghetto," which was weak on beat and strong on slush. It was a No. 1 hit—except in the ghetto—and no doubt met with the approval of the Make Las Vegas Beautiful folks. Now Kirk Kerkorian, who owns the International and apparently wants to become Nevada's other famous tycoon, was energetically promoting Elvis's return to the stage. . . .

The opening took place in the Showroom Internationale, a two-thousand-seat nightclub whose sublimely irrelevant décor included relief carvings of Greek temples and winged gods and goddesses, and whose menu that night consisted of such tasty items as Aloyau Roti à l'Anglaise Périgourdine and Pointes d'Asperges au Beurre. The audience was 99.44 per cent white and predominantly middle-aged and moneyed; the celebrities present ranged from Fats Domino and Phil Ochs to Pat Boone and Henry Mancini. I was surprised at how seriously people were taking the occasion. They seemed to feel that Elvis was theirs, not just a progenitor of the music their kids listened to. A woman of fifty who had come from Los Angeles whispered excitedly, "My husband thinks I'm real silly, but I always wanted to see Elvis in person." It was obviously the raunchy Elvis, not the Hollywood Elvis, that she wanted to see.

We had to sit through the Sweet Inspirations—a great black gospel-rock group that persists in wasting its talent singing "Alfie"—and one of those unmentionable comedians. Then Presley came on, and immediately shook up all my expectations and preconceived categories. There was a new man out there. A grown man in black bell-bottoms, tunic, and neckerchief, devoid of pout and baby fat, skinny, sexy, totally alert, nervous but smiling easily. For some reason, he had dyed his hair black. It was the same length as ever, but combed down instead of back into a ducktail. He started with "Blue Suede Shoes." He still moved around a lot, but in a much different spirit. What was once deadly-serious frenzy had been infused with humor and a certain detachment: This is where it began—isn't it a good thing? Though the show was more than anything else an affirmation of Presley's sustaining love for rhythm and blues—we knew it all the time, Elvis—it was not burdened by an oppressive reverence for the past. He knew better than to try to be nineteen again. He had quite enough to offer at thirty-three. He sang most of his old songs, including a few of the better ballads, and a couple of new ones. When he did "In the Ghetto," his emotion was so honest it transformed the song; for the first time, I saw it as representing a white Southern boy's feeling for black music, with all that that implied. "Suspicious Minds," an earthy country-rock song about jealousy, which is going to be Presley's new single, was the highlight of the show. . . . Elvis was clearly unsure of himself, worried that he wouldn't get through to people after all those years, and relieved and happy when he realized we were with him. As the evening went on, he gained in confidence, and the next night he was loose enough to fool around with the audience, accepting handkerchiefs to mop his forehead and reaching out his hands to women in the front row. During both performances, there was a fair amount of sighing and screaming, but, like Elvis's sexual posturing, it was more in fun than in ecstasy. . . .

If Elvis continues to perform—he says he wants to—and "Suspicious Minds" is as big a hit as it should be, he could have a significant impact on pop music in the coming months. It remains to be seen whether he can transcend either his grand-old-man image or the Hal Wallis years, but he seems to want to try. I wonder if Colonel Parker approves. Is Parker just an ectoplasmic projection of Presley's Hollywood side? Will he now shrivel up? The night before I left Las Vegas, I saw him drop five hundred dollars at roulette. You can't win 'em all.

DOCUMENT 10: THE KING IS DEAD

Elvis's death on August 16, 1977, was met with eulogies in newspapers across the nation. The following two—from the Philadelphia Inquirer *and* Boston Globe, *respectively—are typical in their high praise for Elvis. Dozens of similar homages are available in the book* When Elvis Died, *by Neal and Janice Gregory.*

MUCH MORE THAN A HOUND DOG

He entered the national limelight almost as suddenly as he departed. As his death is officially recorded as Aug. 16, 1977, at the age of 42, his imprint on the national consciousness can be fixed at Sept. 9, 1956, at the age of 21.

With his guitar in hand, his black greasy hair slicked back, pants molded to his legs and hips moving like a spinning top, Elvis Presley made his first appearance on the Ed Sullivan Show, the first of three he was signed for at the whopping sum of $50,000.

It was the 50s, the age of innocence, so the network protected us from the Memphis singer. We were allowed to see everything from the waist up, including his lip slightly curled with contempt.

From the press clippings and from the frenzy screams of his fans in the audience, we knew much more was happening as he sang his four songs—"Don't be Cruel," "Ready Teddy," "Hound Dog" and "Love Me Tender." But that was left to our imagination.

In any event, the era of Elvis, the King of Rock 'n' Roll, had dawned. To his breathless admirers it would last forever. To his critics weaned on Rudy Vallee and Frank Sinatra, it was a fad. After his television appearance, one local critic wrote, "What will happen to Presley when the craze has ended—and all of them end— is anybody's guess of course. But it seems to many that he will be through as an act. And the big reason for that is his voice—to use the word loosely."

To the extent that everything eventually ends the critic was right, perhaps. But 250 million records, 33 films and millions of dollars later, his fans had a far more accurate pulse on the national mood than the pundits.

Elvis didn't invent Rock 'n' Roll anymore than Beethoven invented classical music. Yet, it is hard to imagine the music flourishing if he hadn't been around. There was more to Elvis, however, than his music or his voice—to use the word loosely or not.

He was despised by the older generation, and, thus, revered by the younger. He was a symbol of rebellion, the generation gap. In an age of moderate politics, peace abroad as well as at home, he was, in retrospect, a hint of what was to come—the sexual revolution, fighting in the streets, protests in the universities.

It is no wonder then that his death, sudden as it was, not only reminds us of how mortal we all are but of another time when life seemed simpler. Elvis's gyrating hips and all.

THE ELVIS LEGEND

Elvis Presley's life was an American life. The Horatio Alger story of a $35-a-week truck driver who made millions. The sneering rebel rejected, then embraced by the mainstream. The young man who willingly sacrificed a bit of his career to serve his country. The craftily marketed "star." The conspicuous consumption. The equally conspicuous generosity. The enduring tension between the demands of celebrity and the desire for privacy. And, underpinning it all, a unique and legitimate talent.

In recent years, as the changing styles and substance of rock flashed by, Elvis seemed increasingly an icon from an earlier age. He evinced neither a social conscience nor a social antipathy. In an age of wiry stars, he had a problem with his weight. With jeans and body shirts the uniforms of the day, his gold lame suits and high shirt collars seemed as outdated as high-button shoes. In an age when stars led lives of quiet ostentation, Elvis's Memphis mansion with its regiment of hangers-on and its motorpool of Cadillacs seemed unfashionable, even gauche. And in a time when the Beatles had long since "done it in the road," Elvis's modest pelvic rolls were tame indeed. Like other fading stars of the entertainment arts, Elvis seemed to become almost a parody of himself.

But if pop music passed Elvis by, it traveled on the course he had set. With his DA haircut, his low-slung pants, his undulations, his driving rhythms, his curled upper lip, Elvis led a revolt against the Tin Pan Alley music of the Fifties. Thousands of screaming and adulating fans joined the cause. And it triumphed.

Others sharpened the rock revolt, made its sexual appeal even more overt, added to both the substance of the lyrics and the subtlety of the music, allied it with the broader cultural and political ferment of the time.

With his rebellious pose and his driving style, Elvis had an effect on each succeeding phase. As the song said, rock 'n roll is here to stay—at least its influence is. And with it will remain the legend and legacy of Elvis.

Part I: Reprinted from "Much More than a Hound Dog," *The Philadelphia Inquirer,* August 18, 1977.

Part II: Reprinted from "The Elvis Legend," *The Boston Globe,* August 18, 1977. Reprinted with permission.

DOCUMENT 11: PRESIDENT CARTER'S STATEMENT ON THE DEATH OF ELVIS PRESLEY

The day after Elvis's death, President Jimmy Carter made a public statement of mourning over the nation's loss—a rare honor, especially for an entertainer. Carter credits Elvis with changing "the face of American popular culture."

Elvis Presley's death deprives our country of a part of itself. He was unique; and irreplaceable. More than twenty years ago he burst upon the scene with an impact that was unprecedented and will probably never be equaled. His music and his personality, fusing the styles of white country and black rhythm and blues, permanently changed the face of American popular culture. His following was immense and he was a symbol to people the world over, of the vitality, rebelliousness, and good humor of his country.

Jimmy Carter, statement on the death of Elvis Presley, August 17, 1977.

Chronology

Elvis Aron Presley is born at 12:20 P.M. in East Tupelo, Mississippi. His twin brother, Jesse, is stillborn.

1945

Elvis wins second prize at the Mississippi-Alabama Fair and Dairy Show for singing "Old Shep."

1946

Elvis receives his first guitar. RCA Victor introduces the vinyl plastic phonograph record.

1948

The Presleys move to Memphis, Tennessee, in September.

1950

Sam Phillips founds Memphis Recording Service.

1953

The House Un-American Activities Committee accuses hundreds of Americans of being Communists. In June, Elvis graduates from high school, takes a job as a truck driver, and that summer records "My Happiness" and "That's When Your Heartaches Begin" at Memphis Recording Service.

1954

The Supreme Court rules that segregated schools are unconstitutional. Elvis records several more songs and meets Sam Phillips. On July 7 WHBQ in Memphis plays the first Elvis song on the radio. On July 19 his first record, "That's All Right Mama/Blue Moon of Kentucky," is released and sells twenty thousand copies. On July 30 Elvis makes his first concert appearance. He continues recording and performing for the remainder of the year. In September *Billboard* magazine names Elvis "Most Promising New Artist of the Year," and in October he appears on the local television program *Louisiana Hayride.* In November he quits his job as a truck driver.

1955

Elvis tours throughout the South, and in July meets Colonel Tom Parker for the first time. In the fall radio station WERE of Cleveland becomes the first to play an Elvis record in the North. In November Elvis signs a three-year deal with RCA Victor.

1956

In January "Heartbreak Hotel" is released and by April it becomes Elvis's first number one hit. On January 28, Elvis makes his national television debut on the Dorsey Brothers' *Stage Show.* In March, Parker becomes Elvis's manager and Elvis's first LP, *Elvis Presley,* becomes RCA's best-selling LP ever. On April 1 Elvis signs a three-picture deal with Paramount Pictures, and on April 3 he appears before an audience of 40 million on the *Milton Berle Show.* On April 23, Elvis makes his first appearance in Las Vegas and does not return until 1969. On June 5 he again appears on the *Milton Berle Show* and on July 1 he appears on the *Steve Allen Show.* On August 22, filming begins on Elvis's first movie, *Love Me Tender,* which is released in November. On September 9, an estimated 54 million tune in for Elvis's censored performance on *The Ed Sullivan Show.*

1957

On March 19, Elvis buys Graceland mansion for $102,500 and moves in, with his parents, on April 10. *Loving You* and *Jailhouse Rock* are released. On December 20, Elvis receives his draft notice.

1958

On March 24 Elvis is inducted into the army and on March 28 he arrives at Fort Hood, Texas. On June 4, *King Creole* is released. Gladys Presley dies on August 14. On September 22 Elvis departs for Bremerhaven, West Germany. He arrives on October 1 and is greeted by 1,500 fans. In November Elvis meets Priscilla Beaulieu for the first time.

1960

Elvis leaves Germany on March 2 and is discharged from the army on March 5. On March 22 he receives a black belt in karate. ABC airs *Frank Sinatra's Welcome Home Party for Elvis Presley* on May 12. On October 20 Elvis's first movie since leaving the army, *G.I. Blues,* is released, and *Flaming*

Star follows on December 20. Priscilla Beaulieu spends Christmas at Graceland.

1961–1969

Elvis stars in a total of twenty-five movies.

AUGUST 27, 1965

Elvis and the Beatles meet in Los Angeles.

MAY 1, 1967

Elvis and Priscilla are married in Las Vegas.

1968

Lisa Marie Presley is born on February 1. From June 27 to 29, Elvis records the television special *Elvis* for NBC, which airs on December 3.

1969

From July 31 to August 28 Elvis plays a series of "comeback" performances at the Las Vegas International Hotel. *Charro!, The Trouble with Girls,* and *Change of Habit* are released. "Suspicious Minds" becomes Elvis's last number one hit.

1970

The film *Elvis: That's the Way It Is* is released. Elvis meets President Nixon at the White House in December.

1972

Elvis and Priscilla separate and Elvis files for divorce on August 18. *Elvis on Tour* is released and wins a Golden Globe award for best documentary.

1973

On January 14, *Elvis: Aloha from Hawaii via Satellite* is aired simultaneously in over forty countries. The Presleys' divorce is finalized on October 9.

AUGUST 16, 1977

Elvis dies at the age of forty-two.

JUNE 7, 1982

Graceland is opened to the public.

JANUARY 23, 1986

Elvis becomes one of the first ten people inducted into the Rock & Roll Hall of Fame.

FOR FURTHER RESEARCH

Peter Harry Brown and Pat H. Broeske, *Down at the End of Lonely Street: The Life and Death of Elvis Presley.* New York: Dutton, 1997.

Roy Carr and Mick Farren, *Elvis Presley: The Illustrated Record.* New York: Harmony Books, 1982.

Vernon Chadwick, ed., *In Search of Elvis: Music, Race, Art, Religion.* Boulder, CO: Westview, 1997.

Rose Clayton, ed., *Elvis Up Close: In the Words of Those Who Knew Him Best.* Atlanta: Turner, 1994.

Frank Coffey, *The Complete Idiot's Guide to Elvis.* New York: Alpha Books, 1997.

Robert Daily, *Elvis Presley: The King of Rock 'n' Roll.* New York: Franklin Watts, 1996.

Albert Goldman, *Elvis.* New York: McGraw-Hill, 1981.

Peter Guralnick, *Careless Love: The Unmaking of Elvis Presley.* Boston: Little, Brown, 1999.

———, *Last Train to Memphis: The Rise of Elvis Presley.* Boston: Little, Brown, 1994.

Patsy Guy Hammontree, *Elvis Presley: A Bio-Bibliography.* Westport, CT: Greenwood, 1985.

Jerry Hopkins, *Elvis: A Biography.* New York: Simon and Schuster, 1971.

———, *Elvis: The Final Years.* New York: St. Martin's, 1990.

Ernst Jorgensen, *Elvis Presley: A Life in Music: The Complete Recording Sessions.* New York: St. Martin's, 1998.

Paul Lichter, *The Boy Who Dared to Rock: The Definitive Elvis.* Garden City, NY: Dolphin Books, 1978.

Greil Marcus, *Dead Elvis: A Chronicle of a Cultural Obsession.* New York: Doubleday, 1991.

Dave Marsh, *Elvis*. New York: Thunder's Mouth, 1982.

Patricia Jobe Pierce, *The Ultimate Elvis: Elvis Presley Day by Day*. New York: Simon and Schuster, 1994.

Kevin Quain, ed., *The Elvis Reader: Texts and Sources on the King of Rock 'n' Roll*. New York: St. Martin's, 1992.

Gilbert B. Rodman, *Elvis After Elvis: The Posthumous Career of a Living Legend*. New York: Routledge, 1996.

John Strausbaugh, *E: Reflections on the Birth of the Elvis Faith*. New York: Blast Books, 1995.

Martin Torgoff, ed., *The Complete Elvis*. New York: Delilah Books, 1982.

Fred L. Worth and Steve D. Tamerius, *Elvis: His Life from A to Z*. New York: Wings Books, 1992.

INDEX